THE HEROINES OF ANCIENT PERSIA

KAI KAUS ATTEMPTS TO FLY TO HEAVEN

(From a Persian Manuscript in the Metropolitan Museum of Art, New York)

THE HEROINES OF ANCIENT PERSIA

STORIES RETOLD FROM THE
SHĀHNĀMA OF FIRDAUSI

With Fourteen Illustrations

By

BAPSY PAVRY, M.A.

CAMBRIDGE
AT THE UNIVERSITY PRESS
1930

CAMBRIDGE
UNIVERSITY PRESS

University Printing House, Cambridge CB2 8BS, United Kingdom

Cambridge University Press is part of the University of Cambridge.

It furthers the University's mission by disseminating knowledge in the pursuit of
education, learning and research at the highest international levels of excellence.

www.cambridge.org
Information on this title: www.cambridge.org/9781107487444

First published 1930
First paperback edition 2015

A catalogue record for this publication is available from the British Library

ISBN 978-1-107-48744-4 Paperback

To
MY FATHER
AND
to the Memory of
MY MOTHER

PREFACE

Persia's geographical position has made her from the earliest times to this day the link between the East and the West, and although the great Persian Empire has now passed away, the romance of its history will live throughout the ages. Firdausi in his great epic poem, the *Shāhnāma*, or *Book of Kings*, shows us how, in all pertaining to Persia's historic fame, women have played an important part, and this book has accordingly been devoted to the heroines of Ancient Iran.

In representing these heroines of Firdausi's poem, I have followed, one after another, the order given in the epic itself. The background and setting of the scenes can best be visualised by those who know the poem well, and are acquainted with Persian history, but the appeal of these tales is so universal that they will hold the interest and gain the sympathy of even the chance reader. Above all, they show us that the same qualities of human nature, which touch and fascinate us to-day, have always existed, and it is to Firdausi that we owe our knowledge of the quaint and yet strangely modern characters which he portrays.

In order that the book may be of some use to those who are acquainted with the Persian language, I have appended at the end of each story a reference to the original Persian text. It is to be hoped, moreover, that the Index will prove of use, not only to the specialist in the field of Persian literature, but also to the general reader. The fourteen illustrations, here reproduced, have been especially selected for the book from Persian manuscripts in the Metropolitan Museum of Art, New York. They are fine examples of Persian miniature paintings, Mongolian-Persian in style, and represent the work of celebrated artists of the 16th and 17th centuries A.D.

Before closing these prefatory remarks, I wish to thank my former teacher and ever friend, Professor A. V. Williams Jackson, of Columbia University, New York, and my brother, Dr Jal Dastur C. Pavry, M.A., Ph.D., for kindly reading through the entire manuscript and giving many valuable suggestions. There is one other name which I wish to mention. It is that of my father, Dasturji Saheb Cursetji Erachji Pavry, the distinguished Parsi Orientalist and eminent prelate-scholar, who has ever been my source of inspiration and my helpful adviser. To him do I ascribe all that may be best in my work.

BAPSY PAVRY

London
21 *March* 1929

CONTENTS

Preface . . . . *page* vii

List of Illustrations xi

Transcription & Pronunciation xii

Chapter I. Firdausi & the *Shāhnāma* . . . 1

II. Faranak 5

III. Shahrinaz & Arnawaz 10

IV. Rudaba 14

V. Tahmina 23

VI. Gurdafrid 28

VII. Farangis 31

VIII. Manizha 35

IX. Katayun 42

X. Humai & Bih Afrid 49

XI. Queen Humai 53

XII. Nahid 60

XIII. Rushanak 62

XIV. Gulnar 67

XV. Dilafruz-i-Farrukhpai 75

XVI. Sapinud 80

CONTENTS

Chapter XVII. Gurdya . . . . . *page* 84

XVIII. Shirin 89

XIX. Purandukht 96

XX. Azarmdukht 98

XXI. Epilogue 103

Bibliography 105

Index 107

LIST OF ILLUSTRATIONS

Kai Kaus attempts to Fly to Heaven . . *Frontispiece*

Faridun is about to Slay Zahhak . . *facing page* 10

Zal and Rudaba meet when out Riding . . 14

Tahmina visits Rustam 24

Suhrab in Combat with a Woman in Disguise 28

Siyawush passes through the Fire-ordeal . 32

Imprisoned Bizhan fed by Manizha . . 40

Gushtasp plays Polo with the Emperor of Rum 46

Embellished Page of a Persian Manuscript . 54

Rushanak in the Presence of Alexander . . 62

Recitation of Poems to the Accompaniment of
 Music 70

Bahram marries Sapinud 80

Khusrau arrives at Shirin's Palace . . . 90

Shirin goes to see the Rock-carvings by Farhad 94

TRANSCRIPTION & PRONUNCIATION

The system of transliteration here adopted has been governed mainly by the desire for simplicity. For this reason I have omitted all diacritical marks which would indicate the length of vowels or differentiate between certain consonants in Persian names. These diacritical signs, however, will be found in the very occasional transcriptions from the Persian which are here printed in *italics*.

The accent of all Persian words, with few exceptions, is on the last syllable. The Persian vowels and diphthongs have, in the main, the same value as in Italian. The consonant *g* is always hard, as in "*give*"; *kh* is spirant, as in the Scotch "*loch*"; *gh* is likewise spirant, as in dialectic German "*Tage*"; *zh* is similarly a spirant, as in "*azure*".

THE HEROINES OF ANCIENT PERSIA
Stories Retold from the Shāhnāma
of Firdausi

CHAPTER I

FIRDAUSI & THE *SHĀHNĀMA*

Firdausi was born at Tus in north-eastern Persia about A.D. 935, and came of an old Iranian family of landed proprietors. His claim to fame rests largely on his *Shāhnāma*, or *Book of Kings*, which comprises nearly 60,000 couplets of flowing Persian verse, and where nearly four thousand years of Persia's history is chronicled. The poet seems to have spent thirty-four years of his life on his great work, which he commenced when he was forty and completed just before his death in A.D. 1025. His main aim throughout was to glorify the national history of his fatherland and its folk, whether in myth, story, religious tradition or popular tale.

We learn from Firdausi himself that the material for the *Shāhnāma* had already (about A.D. 640) been embodied in a Pahlavi prose epic, the *Khvatāi-nāmak*, or *Book of Sovereigns*, and that it was a young poet named Dakiki, an early contemporary of his, who first conceived the idea of turning it into verse. No sooner had he commenced the work, however, when he was murdered, and Firdausi, though admitting his inferiority as a poet, took it in hand, and after many setbacks was able at last to carry it through successfully.

Firdausi has followed tradition by dividing the annals into four periods, each marked by a succession of kings. These are (1) the Pishdadian period, from the earliest times to about 1000 B.C.; (2) the Kaianian period from about

1000 B.C. to 330 B.C., and comprising the historic Median (708–558 B.C.) and the Achaemenian (558–330 B.C.) rule; (3) the Ashkanian or Parthian period, from 330 B.C. to A.D. 225; and (4) the Sasanian period, from A.D. 226 to A.D. 651.

I have already mentioned that this book is written to stress the important part played by women in Persian history, as depicted in Firdausi's poem. In the earlier periods of the epic it is natural that the feminine figures are somewhat shadowy, but the poet's touch is not lacking in fancy. Later, when his material was less scanty, his characters become more individualistic and clear-cut. Firdausi, however, at no time forgot either his sympathy or his poetic art in dealing with his female characters. He sought most of all to paint an ideal type of the eternal feminine in Persia, and we may rightly treasure the picture, the outlines of which have been given such an enduring form through his poetic skill

THE PISHDADIAN PERIOD

From the earliest times
to about 1000 B.C.

CHAPTER II

FARANAK

Faranak, daughter of the King of the Scythians, became the wife of Abtin,[1] a descendant of the great Iranian King, Jamshid. She had fallen in love with Abtin when he came to her father's court during his travels.

Shortly before the birth of her son Faridun, Zahhak, the demon-like King of Babylon, who had usurped the throne of Persia, had been terrified by a dream, in which he saw himself taken prisoner and ignominiously dethroned by a kingly and valiant youth. Greatly disturbed in his mind as to the meaning of the vision, he summoned the wisest of his archmages and astrologers. He commanded them to look into the future and foretell what would be his fate. Fearful as to the manner in which he might visit his wrath upon them, the sages were loth to speak until, after three days, his patience exhausted, the King adjured them to "speak or be hanged alive!" Thereupon, the chief of the band stepped forward and interpreted the dream as signifying that a child about to be born and named Faridun was

[1] In the *Avesta*, or *Sacred Book of the Parsis*, we can recognise Abtin (Avestan *Āthwya*) as founder of the noble Zoroastrian Athwyani clan. This throws an interesting sidelight on Firdausi's account, and makes our heroine's choice of so distinguished a husband the more appropriate. For the Avestan passages referring to *Āthwya* and his clan, compare Yasna 9. 7 and Yasht 13. 131.

destined to bring him to ruin. Zahhak, filled with dread, determined to search the world for traces of the infant, and sent forth the chiefs of his army, charging them, in the event of their being successful, to destroy the entire family as well as the child.

Meanwhile, Abtin, the father of Faridun, becoming aware of Zahhak's designs on his son and feeling his own life imperilled, fled from his home, only to fall into the hands of the enemy. He was seized, borne captive to the King and forthwith put to death. Faranak, heartbroken at her husband's cruel fate and terror-stricken for the safety of the child Faridun, fled also from home, carrying the precious infant in her arms, and made her way towards the desert, where, in a distant pasture ground, she descried a beautiful cow—none other than the famous Birmaya, or Purmaya, according to the legend. Overcome, and weeping with fatigue both physical and mental, she besought the owner of the pasturage to nourish her babe with the milk of this wonderful cow.

> "Ask what thou wilt," she cried,
> "E'en to my soul, 'tis thine!"

The good man, moved to compassion at her plight, soothed and comforted her, promising to care for the child as a father. Faridun remained under his faithful guardianship for three years.

Zahhak, however, never wearied of the search, and the beautiful Birmaya becoming more and more talked of, terror again clutched at the heart of Faranak that he might

discover the field where her infant lay hidden. She, therefore, sought the guardian of the child and confided to him
her fears. With many regrets, his kind protector delivered
up the boy, and Faranak fled with him to Mount Alburz,[1]
where dwelt a holy man, to whom she made piteous appeal
"to take the child and father him with care". The holy man
took Faridun and reared him till he grew to be a brave and
handsome youth.

In the meantime, the wicked Zahhak having learned the
story of Birmaya and Faridun, sought out the noble cow,
killed her and all the other cattle in the field, and then proceeded to the house of Faranak. Infuriated at finding it
deserted, he burned the lofty palace to the ground.

When Faridun reached the age of sixteen years, he obtained permission from the holy man to come down from
Mount Alburz to visit his mother. With tears of joy they
met and embraced; but, when Faridun asked to be informed
as to his birth, and Faranak related the tragic history from
beginning to end, he became enraged and vowed he would
wreak vengeance upon Zahhak. Vainly his mother implored
him to abandon his rash schemes, dwelling on the power of

---

[1] The great mountain range of Alburz in northern Persia (Avestan
Harā Berezaitī) plays an important rôle throughout the history of Iran.
Owing to the allusion to Hindustan, we probably must interpret the
mention of Alburz as referring to the eastern end of this mighty range
of the Caucasus. But the poet's geography is not to be enquired into
too closely. Tradition does connect Faridun indirectly with the region
of Sistan through a side line of the royal dynasty. Compare Mohl,
Le Livre des Rois, vol. I, p. 59.

the mighty monarch, against which it were the height of
madness for a mere youth thus to pit himself:

> Drunk with the wine of youth,
> Men think themselves. the only ones on earth
> And vapour, but be thy days mirth and joy.
> Do thou, my son, bear this advice in mind:
> Give all words, save thy mother's, to the wind.[1]

It so happened that the people of Iran had been driven to
desperation by the misrule and tyranny they had been
forced to suffer at the hands of Zahhak; so that, when a
certain man—a humble blacksmith, named Kawa, whose
son had, amongst others, been seized, and was about to be
slaughtered to satisfy a whim—turned upon him and openly
defied him, they were only too eager to rise in rebellion.
Placing themselves under Kawa's leadership, they proceeded to seek out Faridun, who immediately prepared to
join them. Before departing the youth turned to his mother
and addressed her thus:

> I must to battle, but do thou
> Invoke the Lord, thy God,
> Who, in joy and sorrow alike,
> Is ever mindful of thy prayers.

Faranak blessed her noble son, and prayed for him with
all her heart and soul. Faridun, as a valiant leader, succeeded in annihilating the iniquitous ruler Zahhak, thereby
recovering the throne of Iran from the usurper's hand and
bringing peace and happiness once more to a sorely tried
race.

[1] Warner, *The Shāhnāma of Firdausī*, vol. 1, p. 154.

His mother, when informed of her son's victory, fell on her knees and offered heartfelt thanks to the great god Ormazd, and, as a proof of her true and deep gratitude, spent the remainder of her life in the service of humanity, giving generously to the poor and performing many noble acts of mercy and self-sacrifice.

In this story of Faranak and Faridun the poet draws a beautiful picture of a mother's devotion to her child. To quote the words of Firdausi, she is indeed "a glorious dame".[1]

[1] For the original Persian text consult Vullers, *Firdusii*, pp. 40–49.

CHAPTER III

SHAHRINAZ & ARNAWAZ

Of the many evils perpetrated by Zahhak, the "Dragon King", one of the most dastardly was his seizure of the two beautiful Princesses, Shahrinaz and Arnawaz, sisters of Jamshid, the great Persian monarch, whom he had overthrown and subsequently put to death. In the *Avesta*, or *Sacred Book of the Parsis*, we find them alluded to as captives of the monster Azhi Dahaka, or Zahhak. We are told in the *Ardvi Sura Yasht* that Faridun, before setting out to conquer Zahhak, invoked the aid of Ardvi Sura Anahita, the Goddess of Waters. The prayer, from the *Avesta*, is here quoted in translation:

Grant me this boon, O good,
Most beneficent Ardvi Sura Anahita!
That I may overcome Azhi Dahaka,
The triple-jawed, the three-headed, the six-eyed,
And that I may deliver his two wives, Savanghavach and Arenavach,
Who are the fairest of body amongst women,
And the most wonderful creatures in the world.[1]

We are already acquainted with something of Zahhak's history. The preceding chapter narrates briefly his dream, his consultation with the astrologers, and also Faridun's determination to wreak vengeance upon him for having

---

[1] Yasht 5. 34. The first Western scholar to point out the identity of these two heroines, in the *Shāhnāma* and in the *Avesta*, was Darmesteter. See his essay on "Çavanhavāc et Erenavāc" in his *Études Iraniennes*, vol. II, p. 215.

FARIDUN IS ABOUT TO SLAY ZAHHAK

(From a Persian Manuscript in the Metropolitan Museum of Art, New York)

killed his father, Abtin, and his nurse, the beautiful cow Birmaya; how the long-suffering people of Iran, under the leadership of Kawa, the blacksmith, rose in revolt and sought out Faridun, who joined them readily.

Calling upon the name of God, the courageous youth, with his followers, rode forth to seek the palace of Zahhak. All day they pressed on. When night fell they tarried awhile to rest. That night Faridun saw, as it were in a dream, an apparition, a fair and nymph-like maiden, who informed him as to the exact position of Zahhak's apartments, and disappeared. Faridun woke up from his slumber, fell upon his knees, and praised God, seeking His divine guidance.

The following day saw their progress impeded by the River Dijla in Baghdad. Faridun commanded the guard to bring forth boats that he and his army might be borne across; but the guard refused, having received orders from the King to allow no one a boat who could not present a passport. Whereupon, the intrepid youth plunged into the stream, and his comrades, fired by his valiant example, followed suit. Those plucky warriors from the land of Iran urged on their steeds, battling with the tide until triumphant, their spirits at least undamped, they landed upon the opposite bank and proceeded once more in the direction of Zahhak's palace.

It rose before them—a magnificent edifice, designed surely to foster happiness and virtue, its fair portals giving no indication of the foul and diabolical secrets it contained. High above the entrance they perceived the talisman Zahhak had placed there, thinking to draw evil from himself. Faridun approached boldly and hurled it to the ground, then hoisting his own mace marched into the palace and made straight for the royal apartments. But, although he searched diligently, he failed to discover any trace of Zahhak.

He came, however, upon two women, the fairest by far he had ever set eyes on. Moved by their sorrowful and terror-stricken countenances, he questioned them as to the cause of their grief, and discovered them to be the ill-fated Jamshid's sisters, whom he had come to deliver. These fair ones, learning his name and purpose, embraced him with tears of joy and gave him their blessing. In response to Faridun's enquiry as to the whereabouts of the wicked King, they informed him that he had fled towards Hindustan. Consumed with terror by his dream of Faridun, which for ever haunted him, he had sought solace in an orgy of slaughter, bathing himself in the blood of his victims. By such form of sorcery he had hoped to avert the calamity.

Meanwhile, news reached Zahhak of Faridun's invasion of his Babylonian kingdom. In a blind rage he hurried back from Hindustan. Employing a lasso, he climbed to the roof where by dint of skilful manœuvring he was able to obtain a view of the royal apartments. Goaded to fury by the spectacle of his two wives with Faridun seated in their midst, he unsheathed his dagger and crept stealthily in. But Faridun was ready for him. No sooner had his feet touched the carpet than he was seized and completely over-powered. Faridun then bound his limbs securely, bore him to a deep and lonely chasm far away in the mountains and there left him to perish.

Thus ended the reign of that terrible and loathsome ruler, and the throne passed to Faridun, the brave and good, who won in marriage the two beauteous dames he had so gallantly rescued. Shahrinaz became the mother of Salm and Tur, the famous Princes, and Arnawaz the mother of Iraj, a future King of Iran.[1]

[1] For the original Persian text consult Vullers, *Firdusii*, pp. 49–62.

CHAPTER IV

RUDABA

Rudaba, a maiden of surpassing loveliness, was the daughter of Mihrab, King of Kabul, who was a descendant of Zahhak, and Zal was the son of Sam, the ruler of Zabulistan, who had abandoned him as a babe, because his hair had been white from birth. As the legend runs, a fabulous bird called Simurg, discovering the infant wailing on Mount Alburz, had taken pity upon him and brought him up. We are told how, in the years that followed, his father repented and suffered the most bitter remorse for his cruelty, so that when news reached him that the child had survived he was transported with joy. He forthwith named him as his successor and promised, in his supreme gratitude, to deny him no wish of his heart. Zal grew to be a tall and extraordinarily attractive youth, and, being of an ambitious turn of mind, resolved on reaching manhood to make a tour of the empire, including the frontiers of Hindustan.

Arriving near Kabul, King Mihrab came out to welcome him in royal array. Their meeting was celebrated with much pomp and the King was greatly impressed by Zal's personality. During the young man's stay at the palace, he learned of the Princess Rudaba, through one of the courtiers, who described her thus:

ZAL AND RUDABA MEET WHEN OUT RIDING

(From a Persian Manuscript in the Metropolitan Museum of Art, New York)

A damsel beautiful, screened from the view of man,
Her face more radiant is than bright the sun,
From head to foot all ivory she,
Tall like the teak-tree, cheeks like Paradise!
Over her silvery neck hang musky locks,
The tips of which like banded anklets curve.
Her mouth a pomegranate bud, cherries her lips.
Two grains of nard swell on her silvern breasts.
Her eyes shine as narcissus in the girth.
Her lashes stole their hue from the raven's wing.
Her archlike brows, the famed bows of Taraz,
Fragrant as musk and dark as bark of Tuz.
Wouldst ask the moon? That is her beauteous face.
Wouldst seek the scent of musk? It is her hair.
She's Paradise adorned in each detail;
Perfect in grace, in joy and every charm![1]

This description aroused such tumult in the heart of Zal
that he became restless with longing for a sight of the
maiden.

Rudaba, on her part, had become more than a little
interested in Zal, having been present when her parents
were discussing him. She had heard her father describe
him as the greatest hero and the strongest warrior on earth,
dwelling on his singularly attractive personality, which his
snow-white hair but enhanced. She found herself unable to
sleep for thinking of him, and, in her yearning for sympathy, confided the secret to her waiting-maids, who were
shocked at the idea, and assured her that her father would
never give his consent to her marriage with a white-haired

---

[1] I am indebted to my friend and teacher, Professor A. V. Williams
Jackson, for the above translation.

man. She thereupon became angry, declaring passionately
that Zal meant more to her than did the mighty King of
the West or any power on earth. The maids, touched by her
earnestness and her grief, sought means by which to aid her.

One day, as they sauntered down towards the river to
gather roses, they happened to descry Zal's royal tent on
the opposite bank and he, catching sight of the girls,
enquired whence they came. On learning that they were
the Princess Rudaba's maids, his heart beat wildly and,
summoning his attendant, he ordered him to bring his bow.
He strung the bow, wounded a water-fowl on the farther
side of the stream, and then despatched an attendant in a
boat to fetch it. When the boy landed on the other bank he
was questioned by the maids, well aware of the stratagem,
as to the archer who had made so skilful a shot. When he
told them, they proceeded to speak of their Princess and
her wondrous beauty, expressing a wish that Zal should
meet her; thereupon the lad returned swiftly with the information. Zal, overjoyed, sent precious gems to the
damsels as gifts for Rudaba, and they sent back word that
they would contrive a secret meeting between him and the
Princess, whose heart was already set on him. Upon receipt
of the message, Zal seized a boat and speedily joined the
maidens, who made him obeisance and spoke to him of their
mistress in such panegyrics:

> A nonpareil the fair Rudaba is,
> A silvern cypress, both in hue and scent.
> A rose, a jasmine, fair from top to toe.

Tall to surmount Canopus viewed from Yaman.
Luscious the wine her face distils, thou'ldst say,
And every lock of hair hath amber scent.
From dome of silver her locks droop to earth
Like ambush-snares over her rose-like cheeks.
Such hair, plaited with musk and ambergris!
While decked her form with rubies fine and gems
And over all, like coat of woven mail,
Tresses and musky locks fall link to link,
Homage to her the moon and pleiads pay![1]

So it came to pass that, on a certain night, the meeting between the lovers took place. Zal made for a secluded spot beneath the wall of Rudaba's bower, high in the towering castle, and presently Rudaba appeared above, like some enchanting sprite, and breathed his name softly. But the lofty parapet where she stood prevented Zal from seeing her face. He begged to be allowed one glimpse of the fairest face on earth, so she loosened her long, black hair and bade him use her tresses as a rope for ascending. Disdaining to commit such a sacrilege, he but bestowed kisses upon her beautiful locks, and procuring from his servant a lasso cord, he flung it aloft and climbed in haste to the bower of bliss, where the lovers sat and gazed upon each other rapturously. But their hearts grew sore when they realised the obstacles that blocked their pathway to happiness, Zal knowing full well that King Minuchihr of Iran and his own father, Sam, would never consent to their marriage. Despite such opposition, however, he swore he would wed none but

[1] Translation from the original by Professor Jackson, here published for the first time and gratefully acknowledged.

Rudaba, and she, in turn, vowed that she would bestow her hand on none but Zal. Thus they sat, side by side, till dawn broke, when with many embraces and protestations of eternal affection the lovers parted.

As Zal went on his way sadly, he recalled the promise his father had made many years ago when he discovered him on Mount Alburz, and forthwith decided to write and impart to him his precious secret. When Sam received the letter he was torn with misgivings, and sought the advice of his priests and astrologers. After some days had elapsed, these wise men presented themselves at the castle with joyful countenances, and assured him that a union between his son and the Princess was destined to bring nought but good in its train. Sam, therefore, returned a kind and hopeful message to Zal, who hastened to apprise Rudaba of the glad tidings, on receipt of which she promptly despatched a handmaiden with a robe and ring as gifts to her beloved. As the messenger was making her way out of the palace, she was unfortunately caught by the Queen, Sindukht. The handmaiden tried to shield Rudaba; but the Queen forced her to disclose the secret. She had a high opinion of Zal, and was greatly distressed, fearing her husband's anger when he should learn the truth. With trembling voice, she broke to him the news, and the King, almost beside himself with rage, threatened to kill his daughter. Sindukht, however, succeeded in reducing him to a calmer frame of mind.

Meanwhile, Zal's father had approached King Minuchihr

to ask his consent to the marriage, whereupon that monarch became highly incensed, and ordered Sam to get together the army immediately and destroy Kabul and every descendant of Zahhak. Sam heard him coolly, deeming it the better policy, and, with his troops, set forth for Kabul. When this came to the ears of Zal, he went to meet his father, and implored him to make one last effort by writing to the King of Iran in favour of the marriage. Sam took his son's advice, suggesting that the youth himself be the bearer of the missive. So Zal proceeded to Iran, where he was received with all honour. His valour and charming personality instantly won the heart of Minuchihr, and touched by Sam's petition on his son's behalf he gave his consent to the union. The threatened hostilities were, therefore, suspended. Zal returned to Kabul, where the royal wedding was celebrated with festivities that lasted the entire week, and Sam rose to the occasion nobly and generously by bestowing the throne and crown of Zabulistan upon Zal.

Rudaba became the mother of Rustam, the greatest hero in the history of the Persian Kings. Her title to fame thus rests secure in the annals of ancient Iran.[1]

---

[1] For the original Persian text consult Vullers, *Firdusii*, pp. 149–227.

THE KAIANIAN PERIOD
From about 1000 B.C. *to* 330 B.C.

CHAPTER V

TAHMINA

This is the tragic story of Tahmina, the fair Princess of Samangan,[1] who fell madly in love with Rustam, the son of Zal and Rudaba, when he paid a chance visit to her father's court.

Rustam had one day been engaged in the chase in the province of Samangan. Becoming weary, he dismounted and dropped off to sleep. When he awoke, Rakhsh, his favourite horse, had disappeared, which left him no alternative but to make his way on foot to the palace of Samangan, the nearest place at which to seek shelter. A youth, possessed of remarkable valour and distinction, he instantly found favour with the King, who entertained him lavishly and made much of him. That evening, when about to retire to rest, he was suddenly confronted by the Princess Tahmina, who made no secret of her admiration for him, of whose heroic deeds she had heard so much, and vowed she would bestow her hand on none other than the strongest and most handsome warrior in the world. Rustam instantly fell a victim to her beauty and charm, and, having imbibed a large quantity of wine, flung prudence to the winds, and

[1] Guy Le Strange, *The Lands of the Eastern Caliphate*, Cambridge, 1905, p. 427, where evidently this large town, Samangan, is referred to as "Saminkan" or "Siminjan". It is situated east of Balkh in modern Afghanistan.

forthwith obtained permission of the King that he might wed his daughter without delay. In the clear, cold light of dawn, however, he saw his act as a piece of mad and reckless folly. Much as he loved Tahmina, the spirit of adventure had the greater hold upon him, and so, with many bitter tears and heartaches, the lovers parted. As a souvenir of their love, Rustam gave to his bride an armlet, with instructions that, if she became the mother of a son, she should bind the token on the boy's arm, but, if a girl were born, she should twine it in her daughter's hair. At this moment the King entered, bearing the news that Rakhsh had been found, so, with a last fond embrace, Rustam took leave of Tahmina and journeyed to his home in Zabulistan, making no mention of this episode to anyone.

Months passed by and Tahmina gave birth to a son, upon whom she bestowed the name Suhrab. As the child grew, his resemblance to his father became more and more pronounced; of exceptional height and girth, he was far in advance of his playfellows, and, for daring and courage, displayed great prowess. Upon reaching manhood, he became restless to discover the whereabouts of his father, having learned from his mother's lips the pathetic little story. He resolved to spare no effort in his determination to bring the two together once more. Selecting a horse, one of the breed of Rakhsh, he gathered an army, and announced his intention of proceeding to Iran to fight against King Kai Kaus, discover his father and make his mother Queen. Tahmina, though sadly loth to part with her son, felt her

TAHMINA VISITS RUSTAM

(From a Persian Manuscript in the Metropolitan Museum of Art, New York)

heart warm towards the brave, impetuous boy, and could not but give him every encouragement. In order to aid him, she procured for him the services of Zhanda Razm, a man who knew Rustam by sight, and could, therefore, point him out to Suhrab as soon as he saw him.

When King Afrasiyab, the rival ruler of Turan, heard about Suhrab, he feared that, should the father and son unite, they would invade Turan. He, therefore, despatched a large army to Suhrab, in order that Kai Kaus might be obliged to call Rustam to his assistance. He instructed the chiefs that, when Rustam came on the battlefield, they should not let Suhrab know that it was his father whom he would meet. In this way, he hoped, the son might fall by the father's sword. Unaware of the evil designs of Afrasiyab, Suhrab gladly accepted the leadership of the large army, thinking it would only serve to further his cause. He thus set forth towards Iran, and captured the White Castle, which was the first strong outpost on the frontier between Turan and Iran. When this came to the ears of Kai Kaus, the King of Iran, he summoned Rustam from Zabul, and asked him to take command of the army and fight against the army from Turan.

That night a catastrophe occurred. Rustam, disguised as a Turkman, was walking round the enemy's camp, when he happened to catch sight of Zhanda Razm, whom he promptly slew, without giving him a chance to speak. Hence the opportunity for identification, as hoped for by Tahmina, was tragically lost.

It was arranged that Rustam and Suhrab should meet in single combat. In the first fight Rustam was defeated, but in the second, Suhrab was mortally wounded. With his dying breath he gasped out the story of his hopeless quest for his father who, he vowed, would take vengeance upon his son's destroyer:

> "Vengeance comes on me from myself!" he cried.
> "'Twas fate that gave into thy hand the key.
> Of this thou'rt blameless: that the vaulted sky
> Hath raised me up to cast me down so soon.
> My peers in years will speak of me with scorn,
> Because my neck hath come thus to the dust.
> My mother gave me signs to know my sire.
> My love for him hath brought my life to an end.
> Ever I searched that I might see his face.
> 'Tis thus I gave my life through that desire.
> My search—alas!—came to no lucky end:
> My father's countenance I ne'er have seen.
> Yet, shouldst thou become a fish in the sea,
> Or turn, like night, into the musky air,
> Or e'en become in heaven like a star,
> Or blot the brilliant sun out of the world,
> Vengeance on thee my father'll surely take
> When he shall see my pillow is of clay.
> Some one of those renowned warriors
> Will bring the proof to Rustam and the news:
> 'Suhrab's been slain, and cast as a vile thing
> Away, while he was making search for thee'."[1]

With a sudden sickening of the heart, Rustam bent over the young man, and, discovering the armlet, realised the terrible truth.

[1] Jackson, *Early Persian Poetry*, p. 111.

"O! my brave son!" he cried in anguish,
"Approved by all, and slain by me!"

In an overwhelming agony of mind, he swooned, but, upon his regaining consciousness, Suhrab had but kind words for him, beseeching him to stay his grief and make no attempt upon his own life. "'Tis but the ruling of destiny," said the lion-hearted hero, his breath growing fainter each moment, "that which was foredoomed hath come to pass." But Rustam, as he watched the passing of his son, almost beside himself with misery and despair, continued to lament bitterly; nor did the wound heal so long as he lived.

When the news reached Tahmina that Suhrab had fallen by Rustam's sword, she became demented. She smote her beautiful face, tore out her hair and rushed about the palace wailing and shrieking, and weeping wildly she cried:

O! my son! O! my son!
Whom shall I call upon to take thy place?
To whom impart my pain and misery?

She then collected all her wealth and jewels and distributed them amongst the poor, and died within a year of a broken heart, to join her warrior son.[1]

[1] For the original Persian text consult Vullers, *Firdusii*, pp. 434–520.

CHAPTER VI

GURDAFRID

Gurdafrid was the daughter of Gazhdaham, the Iranian chief, who had been renowned for his might and valour, but owing to advancing years, was fast losing his strength.

Father and daughter were in residence at the White Castle when Suhrab, the enterprising young hero, arrived with his Turanian army, captured Hajir, the veteran castellan, and prepared to seize the castle also. Gurdafrid was deeply grieved when she learned of Hajir's misfortune, knowing him to be a warrior of no mean attributes. Tall and strong, beautiful and brave, she retired to her own apartments, donned a suit of armour, and, concealing her luxuriant tresses beneath her helmet, rode off on a charger to the battlefield.

In a voice "like thunder" she challenged the warriors of Turan to meet her in single combat. For a moment it seemed none dared approach her. Then Suhrab rushed forward, and a fierce fight began. Gurdafrid displayed extraordinary skill and dexterity. In anger, not unmingled with admiration for such prowess, Suhrab brandished his sword, and, mustering all his strength, struck at his opponent, tearing open her coat. He then snatched off her helmet, and her long hair billowed down over her shoulders.

Suhrab gazed as if spellbound on the beautiful girl who

SUHRAB IN COMBAT WITH A WOMAN IN DISGUISE

(From a Persian Manuscript in the Metropolitan Museum of Art, New York)

stood before him, her bright eyes twinkling with humour, her red lips smiling derisively. He begged her to desist, which she finally agreed to do, at the same time urging him to keep her identity a secret. She taunted him as to the object of ridicule he would become, when it was known that he had summoned all his courage merely to fight a girl. She, moreover, promised to offer no further resistance, telling him the castle should be his.

On her return, she was met by her father, with his troops. Gazhdaham was overjoyed and filled with pride at the sight of her, having suffered the most terrible anxiety on her account. Though bruised and wellnigh exhausted, the maid's valiant spirit prevailed as, making her way out upon the ramparts, she looked down on the enemy. Suhrab, still mounted on his steed, was startled by the sound of rippling laughter, and, gazing upwards, beheld the fair face of Gurdafrid. At her mocking words, the realisation came to him that he had been cleverly foiled.

> "O warrior of Turan!" she gibed,
> "Why take such pains?
> Be off with you, and give up battlefields."

In a state of wrath amounting almost to frenzy, Suhrab took his departure, swearing to destroy the castle the very next morning.

That same night Gurdafrid and her father escaped by a secret passage which ran beneath the fort, so that, when Suhrab arrived, prepared to storm the portals, he found to his amazement that he had but to open the gates and walk in. He was astounded at finding the place deserted, and his capture of the castle seemed but an empty triumph, since it held not Gurdafrid.

"Woe's me!" he cried,
"The bright moon is beclouded."

Thus ends the story of Gurdafrid, and Suhrab's hopeless love for the brave and dauntless maid, destined by fate to cross his path but once in his sadly brief life.[1]

---

[1] For the original Persian text consult Vullers, *Firdusii*, pp. 450–7.

CHAPTER VII

FARANGIS

When good Prince Siyawush, son of Kai Kaus, King of Iran, left his father's palace in order to escape from his malicious stepmother, Sudaba, he sought refuge in the court of Afrasiyab, King of Turan, and there learned of the fair Princess Farangis.

Piran, a distinguished statesman in her father's court, had spoken unceasingly to Siyawush of her beauty and charm:

> She bettereth the cypress tree in stature;
> Her musky tresses form a sable crown;
> Her parts and knowledge pass her loveliness,
> While wisdom standeth as a slave before her.[1]

Thus he sought to bring about an alliance between Farangis and the young Prince. He played upon the youth's ambitions, dwelling on Afrasiyab's partiality towards him and expressing certainty that he would be in favour of the union. Siyawush confessed himself but too eager, and Piran was delighted, since his own interests would be served thereby. He obtained an audience with the King, who readily gave his consent.

Siyawush and Farangis were much impressed when they beheld each other, and the wedding festivities took place without delay. Afrasiyab appointed his son-in-law ruler of

[1] Warner, *The Shāhnāma*, vol. II, p. 271.

the lands extending eastward from Turan to the realm of the sea of Chin, on which Siyawush erected a magnificent palace, called Siyawushgird, and bestowed on his beloved Farangis every desire of her heart.

Afrasiyab had a brother named Garsiwaz, who became extremely jealous of Siyawush, and endeavoured to poison the King's mind against him at every opportunity. He invented scandalous tales to the effect that Siyawush was in treacherous communication with Iran, and, by means of correspondence, negotiated to destroy Afrasiyab and thus become ruler of Turan. Afrasiyab, enraged, sent a large army towards the province of Siyawush. The iniquitous Garsiwaz, proceeding in advance of the hosts, sought Siyawush and counselled him to flee for his life—a traitorous ruse calculated to bring about his capture. Siyawush, however, suspected nothing, and urged on by the faithful Farangis, was at length persuaded into taking the advice of his betrayer. He parted from Farangis in great despair and woe, and journeyed towards Iran with his forces.

On his way thither, he fell into the hands of Afrasiyab, who would listen to none of his explanations or entreaties. When the news reached Farangis, she went to her father and implored him to spare her husband. But the King's heart was hard, and his daughter's tears failed to move him. Summoning all the wit and eloquence at her command, she brought forth every argument, even dwelling on the futility of imagining that, because he was a King, he was omnipotent. She bade him recall the fate of the tyrant

SIYAWUSH PASSES THROUGH THE FIRE-ORDEAL

(From a Persian Manuscript in the Metropolitan Museum of Art, New York)

Zahhak, and bear in mind that retribution would alike overtake him. Said she:

> The world is fleeting, and is full of sobs and sighs.
> One man, though crowned, it casteth into prison;
> One who ne'er had a crown it maketh king.
> Yet fate hath laid the grave's grip on them both,
> And, in the end, both lie alike in dust.[1]

Afrasiyab, fearful of her prognostications, burst into a fit of bitter anger. Calling his guards, he commanded them to take her by force and lock her in a secret chamber in the castle. He then gave the order to one of his chiefs to stab Siyawush. On learning the fate of her beloved husband, Farangis, broken-hearted and distraught, cursed her father, who forthwith commanded that she be scourged and put to death.

A wail of sorrow arose from the entire country at the news that their fair Princess was to be executed. The people cried out that they would no longer recognise Afrasiyab as their King. Then Piran the Wise went to the monarch and pleaded with him to spare the life of Farangis, since she was soon to be a mother. The King told him he might do with her as he wished. So Piran took her to his home, where his good wife cared for her.

Later, a son was born to the Princess, on whom she bestowed the name Kai Khusrau. Afrasiyab, learning of the event through Piran, became filled with remorse, and besought him to take steps to have the boy brought up in ignorance of his cruelty.

[1] Warner, *The Shāhnāma*, vol. II, p. 318.

Meanwhile, the tragic story of Farangis had travelled to Iran, where much compassion was felt for the unfortunate Princess. Kai Kaus dispatched Giv, one of his chiefs, to fetch her and the child. Farangis received Giv with tears of gratitude, and presented him with Siyawush's suit of mail; then, herself disguised, the three set forth across the River Jihun into Iran.

During her stay at the palace of Kai Kaus, his son Fariburz demanded the hand of Farangis in marriage. She was, at first, greatly troubled in mind, with the memory of Siyawush ever in her heart; but, the union being approved by all, she was finally persuaded into giving her consent. Her son Kai Khusrau later became the King of Iran on the death of King Kai Kaus.[1]

[1] For the original Persian text consult Vullers, *Firdusii*, pp. 529–671.

CHAPTER VIII

MANIZHA

In the territory of Irman, which lay between Iran and Turan, the people suffered terribly from the ravages committed by wild boars, and brought a petition to King Kai Khusrau, urging him to send some brave warrior to destroy them. At first no one dared volunteer; then a brave youth named Bizhan stepped forward, and accompanied by Gurgin, a warrior selected by the King to be his guide, set forth on the hazardous enterprise.

Bizhan slew the boars one after another, and Gurgin, realising the fame that would be his, became filled with envy. He forthwith set himself to devise some scheme to blight the young man's career. He told him of the beauty of Manizha, daughter of King Afrasiyab, and urged him to go on to Turan and see her. Bizhan yielded readily to the suggestion, and the two proceeded on their way.

Gurgin halted at some distance from Turan, leaving Bizhan to go forward alone. Arrived there, he took up his stand beneath a cypress tree, in full view of Manizha's tent, where with her handmaidens she was feasting and making merry. Suddenly the fair Princess caught sight of him, and, being very young and fanciful, wondered as to whether so handsome and princely a youth were human or had come from fairyland. She forthwith dispatched her nurse to enquire his name. The nurse returned with the information that his name was Bizhan, and that he had journeyed into Turan for the purpose of beholding her beauty. Manizha, who had fallen in love with him at sight, then invited him into her tent, where they spent many a happy hour together. When night came on and he prepared to depart, the young Princess became very sad, for she did not want him to go. She then bethought her of a drug which, mixed with wine, would temporarily deprive him of his senses. By this means and by dressing him in a woman's garb, she and her hand-maidens bore him in a litter to the palace and concealed him in her apartments. When Bizhan awoke the next morning and discovered the trick which had been played upon him by Gurgin, he cursed him bitterly, but soothed by Manizha's soft words he grew happy and merry in her company.

After a few days, the rumour reached King Afrasiyab that a stranger from Iran was concealed in his daughter's apartments. He became furious, and ordered Bizhan before him. On learning his identity, he condemned him to death. Just as the execution was about to take place, Piran, the grand vizir, arrived on the scene and begged that it be post-poned for a few moments. The kindly official felt sorry for the young man, and pleaded with Afrasiyab to spare his life, pointing out that the youth's destruction would but cause the King of Iran to seek revenge upon him. Afrasiyab was, therefore, persuaded into changing the sentence of death to one of imprisonment. Summoning his guards, he com-manded them to seize Bizhan and confine him in a dark, gloomy pit in a neighbouring forest, closing the opening with a very heavy stone. He then sent for Manizha, and banished her from the palace, driving her forth barefoot, dressed as a beggar. The King's brother led her to the pit and brutally apprised her as to the fate of her lover, whose drudge she should now become. Manizha wept tears of blood as she pictured Bizhan's misery. Day after day she wandered wailing from house to house, begging for food, which she passed to Bizhan through a crevice.

Meanwhile, Gurgin awaited Bizhan's return, and began to fear that some disaster had overtaken him. He became a prey to remorse for the treacherous part he had played, and yearned for a sight of him. But he sought him in vain, and, in despair, returned at last to Iran. When King Kai Khusrau and Giv learned that Gurgin had returned alone, they sent for him and demanded to know what had happened. In desperation, Gurgin invented a story of Bizhan's having been carried off by a wild ass. His face, however, betrayed the lie, and he was immediately cast into prison and threatened with death, should Bizhan not be found.

The first day of the year, the day of Spring Equinox, having arrived, Giv advised King Kai Khusrau to look into the glorious gazing-cup. This was a wondrous vessel in which, on Noroz, or New Year's Day, the King could behold reflected the condition of anyone whom he wished to see. On this occasion the cup revealed to his gaze that Bizhan was imprisoned in a dark pit in Turan, attended by a noble maiden, and that both were weeping bitterly and wishing for death. The King at once summoned Rustam, and urged him to go to Bizhan's rescue, since he was the one warrior in the world qualified to undertake such a task. Rustam consented, and the King gave him a large army and immense wealth.

Arriving on the outskirts of Turan, Rustam stopped his troops at some distance from the border-line and bade them remain there until he needed them. He then entered Turan disguised as a wealthy merchant from Iran. Making straight for the palace, he visited Piran and presented him with precious gems. Piran was exceedingly gratified, and promised that no harm should come to him. The news of the arrival of the merchant from Iran spread through the country and came to the ears of Manizha. She hastened to the warehouse of the merchant, and, after a few preliminary words of courtesy, laid before him Bizhan's sorrowful plight. She questioned him as to his possible acquaintance with King Kai Khusrau and with Giv and Gudarz. Rustam, fearing someone might overhear her conversation with him, shouted at her that he knew nothing of the warriors mentioned. Manizha then burst into tears and told him her own pitiful story. She entreated the supposed merchant to seek out gallant Giv and hero Rustam on his return to Iran, and to urge them to come and release Bizhan, adding that if they tarried Bizhan would surely die. Rustam soothed her, though still concealing his identity, and provided her with a large quantity of food for the prisoner. The most choice delicacy among the consignment was a roasted bird, into which he had quietly slipped his own signet ring.

Swiftly back to the pit she ran, with the food and the intelligence regarding the wealthy "merchant" from Iran, which heartened them both considerably. Bizhan began to eat, and duly discovered the ring with Rustam's name engraved upon it. He knew then that his sufferings would soon be at an end, and he laughed aloud for joy. Manizha, hearing him, was frightened, thinking he had lost his reason. She demanded to know the occasion for such laughter, and he said he would tell her something if she would take solemn oath to keep it a secret. Manizha was profoundly hurt by this seeming mistrust of her, and reproached him bitterly:

> My world is darkened and mine eyes are dim,
> For he concealeth secrets thus from me!

Bizhan immediately grew penitent, as he remembered all her goodness to him. He begged her to forgive his thoughtlessness, saying that his brain must have weakened through suffering. He then told her about the ring, and requested her to go to the merchant and ask him whether he was the lord of Rakhsh.

Manizha hastened to do his bidding, when, to her great surprise, the merchant revealed himself as Rustam in disguise, but impressed upon her the need for absolute secrecy. He told her to light a fire at night, that he might know the exact spot where the pit was located. Once more she sped like the wind back to Bizhan, with the joyful news that the merchant was none other than the gallant warrior Rustam, who had come to rescue him.

When night fell, she kindled a beacon-fire near the pit, and Rustam, on his charger Rakhsh, rode up, accompanied by seven other warriors whom he commanded to remove the stone. Its weight, however, proved so terrific that all their efforts were fruitless. Praying God to grant him strength, the dauntless Rustam lent his aid, and, eventually, the great stone yielded and came away, the earth shaking with the force of it.

Before releasing Bizhan, Rustam extorted from him a promise that he would not seek revenge on Gurgin, but let him go in peace. Though naturally loth to agree to this after all he had endured through Gurgin's treachery, Bizhan at length gave his word. Rustam then hauled him up, and the mighty warrior wept aloud at the spectacle of the once handsome youth—in iron fetters, his hair and nails grown long, his features wan and ghost-like, he was indeed a sorry sight.

Taking Bizhan and his devoted Manizha back to his house, Rustam made plans to attack Afrasiyab the very next day. The battle was fought in the neighbourhood of Mount Bistun,[1] where Rustam gained the victory and Afrasiyab was forced to flee for his life. Rustam then returned in triumph to Iran, bringing with him Manizha and Bizhan. King Kai Khusrau gave them a royal welcome, and held a great feast in their honour. His heart went out to the

[1] Also called Bisitun, Behistun, or *Bagistāna*, that is, "Place of God". It is a lofty rock a few miles east of Kirmanshah and famous for the inscriptions of the great Persian kings of the Achaemenian dynasty.

IMPRISONED BIZHAN FED BY MANIZHA

(From a Persian Manuscript in the Metropolitan Museum of Art, New York)

unfortunate Manizha when he learned of all she had suffered, and of how nobly she had stood by Bizhan. He bestowed on her beautiful garments of brocade, many jewels, a precious crown, slave girls and enormous wealth. He then admonished Bizhan in that he should fully appreciate her heroism and be proud to go through life by her side. Bizhan, however, needed no such admonition, for his love had been ever with her.[1]

[1] For the original Persian text consult Vullers-Landauer, *Firdusii*, p. 1137.

CHAPTER IX

KATAYUN

The story of Katayun, Kitabun, or Nahid, in the *Shāh-nāma* has a peculiar interest, because this daughter of the King of Rum[1] married Gushtasp, or Kava Vishtaspa of the *Avesta*, who later became famous as the patron of Zoroaster's religion. The fair Princess Katayun[2] was the eldest of the three daughters of the sovereign of the west, the Kisra of Rum, as told in the introductory lines of Firdausi's account of Luhrasp, father of Gushtasp, who succeeded Kai Khusrau to the throne of Iran. The Kisra of Rum, we are told, was a descendant of Salm, son of Faridun and Shahrinaz. A union through a royal marriage, that would bring Iran and Rum into closer connection, is a happy theme, and Firdausi develops the romantic story, describing how this beauty from the west became the wife of Gushtasp, son of King Luhrasp.

Luhrasp was very fond of the grandsons of Kai Kaus, in consequence of which the heroic young Gushtasp suspected

---

[1] That is, Asia Minor, the territory which later came to be known as the Eastern Roman Empire.

[2] According to the *Avesta*, however, the name of Vishtaspa's wife was Hutaosa, who belonged to the noble house of the Naotaras; compare Yasht 15. 35. It may be noted here that the romantic episode of Vishtaspa's youth, told by Firdausi and repeated by Mirkhond in his *History* (tr. Shea, pp. 263, 266), is not to be found either in the *Avesta* or the later Pahlavi writings.

that his father might give the throne to one of them. He
was, therefore, greatly troubled. One day, when the King
was feasting the nobles, Gushtasp joined the party, and all
made merry and drank freely. In the midst of the rejoicing,
the youth turned suddenly to his father and asked him to
bestow the throne upon him. The King replied that he was
too young, whereupon Gushtasp became filled with anger
and quitted the court, leaving Iran for Rum.

It was the custom in Rum, when a Princess reached
marriageable age, to assemble all the Princes and Noblemen
that she might choose a husband from among their number.[1]
At a given time the Princess would enter, but surrounded
so completely by her handmaidens that her suitors could
obtain no possible glimpse of her. The night before such
an assembly was to be held for Katayun, she dreamed that
among the noble gathering was seated a handsome young
man of kingly bearing, whom she forthwith selected as her
husband, in token whereof she gave him a bouquet of sweet-
scented flowers. The following morning she awoke, greatly
excited. Procuring a bunch of fresh narcissi, she entered
the grand assembly of Princes, but she saw not one amongst
them whom she liked. Filled with disappointment that her
dream had not come true, she withdrew to her apartments
and wept bitterly.

The next day the King summoned another gathering,

---

[1] This method of contracting marriage was known in ancient India
as *swyamvara*, "self choice" or "maiden's choice"; see *Mahābhārata*,
Adi Parva, §§ CII, CXII.

this time not of Princes, but of wealthy Nobles, hoping
that one of them might prove sufficiently attractive to win
the love of Katayun. To this second assembly came Gushtasp at the advice of the kindly village chieftain, who had
befriended him since he left his father's palace. "Come!"
said that good man, "the sight of so much beauty and
splendour may perhaps cheer thy sad, young heart." He
further advised him to assume the name of Farukhzad,
deeming it more prudent.

At the appointed hour Katayun again entered with her
bouquet of narcissi. Glancing round, she suddenly caught
sight of Gushtasp. Her heart gladdened as she recognised
in him the hero of her dream. She approached him joyously
and "set the rich and splendid coronal upon his glorious
brow", receiving from him a token of love in return.[1]
Neither Katayun nor her father, however, was aware that
the suitor who had won her hand was of royal blood. The
King was, in fact, extremely angry at his daughter's choice
of the stranger, and said he would behead both of them.
The minister, Katayun's tutor, however, intervened, re-
monstrating with him severely: "Thou didst but say to thy

---

[1] A similar romantic episode is preserved in Athenaeus (19. 275 a),
as narrated by Chares of Mitylene. The lover Zariadres (presumably
Zarir), brother to Hystaspes of Media (presumably Gushtasp), was
seen in a dream by the Princess Odatis, whom he later married. Chares
states that the Greeks in Alexander's train had heard the Persians
singing the romantic tale, and adds, "they have represented the story
in paintings in their temples and palaces, and even in their own private
houses"; see Jackson, *Early Persian Poetry*, pp. 6–8.

daughter: 'Choose a husband'. She hath obeyed, and chosen one to her liking. Submit thyself to the will of God". The King accordingly withdrew the sentence of death, but, his anger still unabated, he banished the young couple from the palace, without money, jewels or possessions of any kind. Fortunately, Katayun had on her person a few rare gems and trinkets, and from the proceeds of these they contrived to live in a meagre way. They made their home in the village, and Gushtasp passed his days in hunting.

Some time later Katayun's sisters were sought in marriage by two noble youths. When one of them, Mirin, a Ruman chief, asked the King for the hand of his daughter Dilanjam, he promised to give his consent if he could perform a deed of great prowess: namely, to kill the monster-wolf that roamed the forest of Faskun to the terror of everybody. Mirin departed, sorely perplexed, and studied his horoscope, where he saw, knitted together with his own fortunes, a bold young warrior from Iran, who would become the son-in-law of the Kisra. Mirin, having heard the story of Gushtasp and his marriage with Katayun, went to seek him in the village, where he had already become famous for his remarkable daring and personality. When he learned the object of Mirin's visit to him, Gushtasp immediately repaired to the forest, and succeeded in slaying the wolf. In his intense gratitude, Mirin proceeded to shower gifts upon him, but Gushtasp refused to accept anything. Returning to the palace, the young man went straight to the King and claimed that he had slain the wolf. The Kisra, beholding the

dead monster and struck by such bravery, at once bestowed
his daughter upon Mirin.

When Ahran, another Ruman chief, wished to marry his
youngest daughter, the King made a condition still more
hazardous. He suggested that the youth should kill the
hideous dragon that infested Mount Sakila. Ahran sought
the advice of Mirin, who told him the truth concerning the
slaying of the wolf. He also asked Gushtasp's help, and
that dauntless warrior, ever eager for the most perilous
enterprise, promptly consented. After days of toil Gushtasp
succeeded in tracking down the dragon and killing it.
Having on an impulse extracted the monster's teeth, he
delivered the carcass over to Ahran, who bore it in triumph
to the King. He was instantly rewarded by receiving the
hand of the fair Princess, and the monarch was filled with
pride at having secured two such valiant sons-in-law.

Some time later, the Kisra arranged for a display of polo
and archery to be held in the riding-field attached to the
palace, in which the bravest of the youths were to take part.
Katayun, the keen-witted, persuaded her husband to go and
see the exhibition. Gushtasp watched the polo. After a
while he asked for a stick and ball and joined the players.
His marvellous strokes, delivered one after another, so
startled the players that they dared not renew the game.
Next appeared the gallant knights for archery, and Gushtasp
again came forward. Wielding his bow and arrow, he displayed such wonderful prowess, that the King's curiosity
was roused. Turning to his followers, he asked:

GUSHTASP PLAYS POLO WITH THE EMPEROR OF RUM
(From a Persian Manuscript in the Metropolitan Museum of Art, New York)

Whence is this cavalier?
Call him that I may ask him who he is—
An angel, or a mortal seeking fame.

Gushtasp was, therefore, summoned to the Kisra's presence,
and, upon questioning him, the monarch was astounded to
learn that he was none other than the young man he had
expelled from his palace. Gushtasp reproached him bitterly
for his harshness towards his daughter. He further revealed
that it was he who had slain the wolf and the dragon, and
proved his claim by producing the teeth of the latter.
Feeling much indignation against Mirin and Ahran, and
repenting of his own conduct, the King immediately sought
his daughter and begged her forgiveness. Convinced that
there was some mystery in connection with "Farukhzad", he
proceeded to interrogate her, but Katayun could tell him
nothing.

His true identity was, however, soon to be established,
for, a short time later, King Luhrasp sent from the east his
other son, Zarir, or Zairivairi of the *Avesta*, to ask Gushtasp
to return to Iran and take possession of the throne. Thus,
for the first time did Katayun and her father, the sovereign
of the west, know that the valiant youth was none other
than Gushtasp, heir to the throne of Iran.

Zarir succeeded in persuading his brother to return, the
Kisra having obtained forgiveness of the royal Prince for
the past unpleasant events and bestowed upon Katayun a
dowry of great riches. Gushtasp and Katayun, accompanied
by Zarir, departed in great pomp for the land of Iran. Upon

their arrival, the aged King Luhrasp placed the crown of
sovereignty upon the head of Gushtasp, and passed the
remaining days of his life in pious meditation and worship.
Katayun became the Queen of Iran, and ruled long over
the destinies of the great land.

The most outstanding event in the history of Iran, and
the most glorious occurrence in the long and prosperous
reign of Gushtasp, was the coming of Zarduhsht, or Zoroaster, the prophet of ancient Iran (660–583 B.C.). After considerable hesitation, the King accepts the new evangel, and
later becomes the Constantine of the faith. Space will not
allow us to narrate fully the events which led up to the con-
version of Gushtasp to the new religion. The entire family,
the Nobles of the realm and the people of Iran followed the
example of their ruler, and the new faith soon began to
spread beyond the borders of Iran, especially under the
leadership of Asfandiyar and Bishutan, the two noble sons
of Gushtasp. Turan, the traditional foe of Iran, was once
more on the war-path, this time in the name of the "old
gods". Gushtasp accepted the challenge, and defeated
Arjasp, or Arejataspa of the *Avesta*, the King of Turan,
after severe fighting and considerable loss of life. Among
the Iranian worthies slain was Zarir, the valiant brother of
Gushtasp.[1]

[1] For the original Persian text consult Vullers-Landauer, *Firdusii*,
pp. 1457–94.

CHAPTER X

HUMAI & BIH AFRID

The story of the Princesses Humai and Bih Afrid, although possessing fewer elements of romance than that of their royal parents, Gushtasp and Katayun, is nevertheless interesting and dramatic.

When Gushtasp adopted the religion of Zoroaster, as told in the preceding chapter, the Turanian King, Arjasp, invaded Iran three times. On the first occasion he was defeated, after which Gushtasp, feeling a longing for peace and quiet, resolved to retire into Sistan for a few years. Some time previously he had had his son Asfandiyar unjustly imprisoned. During the absence of Gushtasp and the confinement of Asfandiyar, however, Arjasp seized the opportunity of starting another war. This time he was victorious, carrying away as prisoners the two Princesses, Humai and Bih Afrid. When the terrible news reached Gushtasp, he hastened back to Iran to make war upon Arjasp; but that monarch came to meet him with so mighty an army that he was hopelessly defeated, and fled to the mountains, where he hid himself in a cave. While concealed there, he sent the wise vizier, Jamasp, to implore Asfandiyar to deliver his sisters from Arjasp. Jamasp departed on his errand to the prison, where Asfandiyar heard him with a show of callousness. He spoke of his sisters in terms of the bitterest reproach, saying that, since Humai had never even thought to visit him in prison, and Bih Afrid, he was sure, cared not whether he were dead or alive, why should he, in his turn, concern himself with them; and, as for his father, if he could put his son into prison, he could surely know how to deliver his daughters. Jamasp, however, continued to plead with him, till Asfandiyar, who was at heart a brave and gentle youth, yielded at last to his entreaties, determining at the same time to avenge the death of his beloved uncle Zarir, who lost his life in the first Holy War.

On being released from his bonds, Asfandiyar immediately sought his father, who embraced him with tears in his eyes, and offered him his crown and throne if he would but rescue his sisters. Asfandiyar forthwith gathered an army, and proceeded to Turan. Arriving on the outskirts, he bade his troops remain in hiding, and, according to plan, entered the country disguised as a rich merchant named Kharrad. There he opened a shop, as if to do business.

It chanced that one evening as the sun was setting, Humai and Bih Afrid were sent from the palace to perform the menial task of fetching water from the well in the town. As they made their way sadly down the street, bearing pitchers upon their shoulders, they came upon the shop of the "merchant" from Iran, before which they stopped. Asfandiyar, catching sight of them, instantly recognised his sisters, and hid his face from them. They entered the shop and approached him, the tears streaming from their eyes, and laid before him their pitiful plight, begging him to aid them if he could. Asfandiyar listened with the uttermost compassion, and began to speak soothing words, but Humai at once recognising her brother's voice, the secret was out. He, however, impressed upon them both not to reveal his presence, telling them he had come there to rescue them. They returned to the palace blessing their valiant brother.

Asfandiyar then proceeded with the second stage of his plan. He went to King Arjasp and informed him that, while on shipboard on his way to Turan, a fierce storm had arisen, and that he had sworn to God that if he reached Turan safely, he would give a great feast as an act of thanksgiving. He forthwith obtained the necessary permission from the King, requesting him to send all the chiefs of his army as guests. Arjasp, suspecting nothing, graciously complied. Asfandiyar then proposed that the feast be held out on the ramparts, saying that it would be a pity to turn the castle into a scene of revelry and disorder; he further suggested lighting a fire out there to gladden the hearts of the nobles; and the King readily consented to these arrangements.

All the chiefs went to the feast, and drank wine freely, so that in a very short time, they were quite intoxicated. A cloud of smoke arose from the fire, and this was the signal which had been arranged by Asfandiyar for the attack by his forces.

The army instantly came up and surrounded the fort, whereupon Asfandiyar, "roaring like a lion", rushed into the King's palace. On hearing him, his sisters hurried out to join him. He bade them repair to his warehouse and wait there until the battle was over. He then hastened to

4-2

the royal apartments, slew Arjasp and took possession of the castle.

It was thus that the valiant Asfandiyar delivered his two fair sisters and brought them safely back to their father in the land of Iran.

> Such is the fashion of life's changeful day!
> Thou hast by turns its sweetness and its bane.
> Why dote upon this Hostel by the Way?
> Grieve not, thou canst not, as thou know'st, remain.[1]

This episode reminds us somewhat of the rescue of Shahrinaz and Arnawaz from the evil Zahhak by Faridun. We may also compare it with the Hindu epic *Rāmāyana*, where Ravana carries away Sita, to be rescued by her valiant husband Rama, and indirectly, with the rescue of Helen of Troy in the Homeric legend. The disguise of Asfandiyar as a merchant from Iran reminds us of a similar stratagem employed by Rustam in rescuing Bizhan and incidentally Manizha.[2]

[1] Warner, *The Shāhnāma*, vol. v, p. 154.
[2] For the original Persian text consult Vullers-Landauer, *Firdusii*, pp. 1613–21.

CHAPTER XI

QUEEN HUMAI

Humai[1] was the first and by far the greatest of the three queens, who, according to the partly legendary and partly historical dynastic scheme of the *Shāhnāma*, ruled over Iran in ancient times.

This beautiful and intelligent Princess married the Iranian King Bahman,[2] who some few months later became seriously ill. Feeling the approach of death, he summoned all the members of his family, together with the nobles and chiefs, and expressed a desire that Humai should rule until such time as she had a son or daughter of age to take over the sovereignty. Shortly afterwards he died, and Humai succeeded to the throne. Her first act, on being declared Queen, was to open her treasury and lavishly distribute her wealth among all equally. She determined, wherever possible, to right wrong, help the poor, and establish peace and prosperity throughout the land.

---

[1] She is also known by the name of *Cihrāzād*, which means "Noble-born", or "Of-noble-mien".

[2] This Bahman is *Vohūman Ardashīr Dīrāzdast* of the Pahlavi books, and there are historical grounds for connecting his long reign of 112 years with that of Artaxerxes Longimanus (465–425 B.C.) and that of his successors. Consequently, Humai, both in the Pahlavi and Persian accounts, may be regarded as semi-historical. See Jackson, *Zoroaster*, pp. 158–61, and particularly p. 160, where notice is taken of Dr West's suggestion that she may possibly be Parysatis.

If the excellent Humai possessed one weakness, it was
love of power. So dear to her was the sovereignty that
when some time later a son was born to her, she concealed
the infant, giving out word to the people that it had died
at birth. When the child was eight months old, he showed
promise of developing into a fine sturdy boy bearing a
striking resemblance to King Bahman, and Humai's jealous
fears grew as she regarded him. She then bethought her of
a plan by which to dispose of him. She sent for a skilful
carpenter, and bade him build a miniature ark, choosing
the finest materials, and lining it with brocade of Rum.
When completed,

> She placed within a pillow for a bed,
> And filled it full of pearls of splendid water.
> They poured in quantities of ruddy gold,
> Mixed with cornelians and emeralds.[1]

Then, on the infant's arm she bound a wondrous jewel
"such as kings might wear", and when midnight came, the
nurse was sent to deposit him in the ark. She wrapped him
warmly in fine silk, and, heartbroken and tearful, did as she
was bid, setting the ark adrift upon the River Farat.[2]

When dawn broke, a washerman carrying on his trade
at an inlet of the stream, was startled at the sight of the
beautiful little craft floating towards him. He recovered it,

---

[1] Warner, *The Shāhnāma*, vol. v, p. 295.

[2] In the Arab geographies the Euphrates is called the *Farāt*. If
Firdausi's geography has real background here, it might be taken to
show the extent of the Persian empire at this time; but no special stress
may be laid on this point.

EMBELLISHED PAGE OF A PERSIAN MANUSCRIPT

(From a Persian Manuscript in the Metropolitan Museum of Art, New York)

and, beholding the babe inside quickly swathed the ark in
a heap of clothes he had been washing, and hurried into the
house in search of his wife. At first, the good woman began
to scold him for not attending to his work; but, when he
unwrapped the bundle and showed her the treasure it contained, her ill-humour gave place to ecstasy, and both gazed
rapturously on the infant and the gold and gems which surrounded him. They wondered greatly as to whom such a
babe could belong. A king's son, forsooth! There was,
however, no means of finding out, and these humble folk
longed for a child, having lost the only one they had. They
therefore adopted the infant as their son, and named him
Darab, because they found him in the water.[1] Some time
later they deemed it advisable to move to another city,
where they sold a large proportion of the jewels, and were
thus enabled to live in happiness and prosperity with their
beloved foster-child.

Darab grew to be a splendid youth, full of strength and
daring. His fondness for the bow and arrow nevertheless
caused his father much annoyance. In vain he endeavoured
to interest the lad in his trade, Darab protesting that such
work was not for him. Feeling a desire to learn the *Avesta*,
or the *Sacred Scriptures*, he asked his father to procure for
him a tutor, and the good man immediately complied with

---

[1] This is the popular etymology to explain the name, as if derived
from *dār* and *āb*, and to mean "Recovered-from-water". This is undoubtedly Darius II of real history (425–405 B.C.), some of the inci-
dents of whose reign will be described in the next chapter.

this request. Later, he expressed a wish to become a knight, and this wish also was gratified, his loving foster-father selecting as his instructor one who was highly skilled in horsemanship.

As he grew older, Darab became more than ever convinced that these humble people were not his parents, and one day he took a sudden resolution. As soon as the washerman had departed to his work, he made fast the door, and, brandishing a scimitar, ordered his mother to tell him who he was. The terrified woman then told him the whole story of how he had been found. Darab was amazed, and demanded to know whether she had any of the money or jewels. She showed him her store amongst which was a large uncut ruby, and placed all at his disposal saying that she and her husband lived but for him. Darab then purchased a horse and became a wonderful rider.

Meanwhile, peace and happiness had prevailed in Iran under the rule of the good and just Queen Humai, when suddenly news was brought to her that an army was coming from Rum to invade the country. She, therefore, ordered the warrior Rashnavad to gather an army and lead it towards Rum. Darab, learning of this, enrolled his name on the list of the troops. When the army was fully mustered, the Queen came out to review the host and to supervise the registration and the numbering of the men. As the soldiers came towards her, she suddenly caught sight of Darab seated upon his steed with kingly grace. Greatly impressed by his handsome face and lofty bearing, she wondered as to his identity and pondered long upon him, until, having given instructions that they should keep her informed as to their progress, the troops took leave of their Queen and marched through the desert towards Rum.

One night a terrific storm arose; the rain poured down and flooded the earth, which shook with the force of the thunder. Rashnavad the general was, therefore, compelled to order a halt and bid his men seek refuge until the tempest abated. Darab, glancing wearily around him, espied a ruined edifice, and making his way under the vaulted dome sank down and dropped off to sleep. Some time later, Rashnavad, happening to pass the ruins on his round, was startled at the sound of a strange voice proceeding from the desert:

> O ruined vault! be very circumspect!
> Be careful of the monarch of Iran.
> He had not any shelter, friend or mate,
> And so he came and sheltered under thee.[1]

Extremely perplexed, and not a little afraid, he stood and listened, and again heard the voice:

> O vault! close not the eye of wisdom,
> For 'neath thee is the son of Shah Bahman.
> Fear not the rain and keep these words in mind.[1]

Wondering greatly, Rashnavad remained as if rooted to the spot, until the voice was heard a third time; then, calling some of his men, he commanded them to search the vault. They entered the ruins and a moment later returned with Darab. No sooner had they done so than the lofty structure

[1] Warner, *The Shāhnāma*, vol. v, p. 303.

collapsed. All were astounded at the youth's miraculous escape, while Rashnavad, after his singular experience, could not but regard it as deeply significant. At the first opportunity, he questioned Darab, and learned from his lips his strange history. The general now procured for him a change of raiment, set him upon an Arab steed and gave him a gold-sheathed sword. He then despatched a messenger to fetch the washerman and his wife. At day-break, he appointed Darab leader of the troops, when they resumed their march and attacked the army of Rum. Darab fought like a lion, and slew the Ruman warriors by hundreds, winning the admiration of the Kisra by his bravery.

Crowned with complete victory, they returned in triumph to Iran. The washerman and his wife had appeared tremblingly in the region of the ruined vault to answer Rashnavad's summons. They corroborated the story of Darab, and received from the kindly general words of high praise for their goodness to the foundling. Arriving within the borders of Iran, Rashnavad wrote a letter to the Queen, giving her the details concerning Darab, and enclosing the few jewels that remained, among which was the gem she had herself bound on his arm. On receiving this intelligence, Humai was very much affected, and recognised at once the young hero as her son. She sent for him and embraced him, bitterly regretting her act and scarcely hoping for his forgiveness. But the generous-hearted youth made light of what he termed his mother's one fault. Humai then prepared for him a gorgeous throne, and, beholding him seated there, her eyes filled with wonder and love. Summoning the entire court, she announced that he was the son of Bahman, and now their King, and much jubilation and rejoicing ensued.

Darab's first thought, on attaining the sovereignty, was of the faithful washerman and his wife. As a reward for all their kindness, he bestowed on them riches and many jewels, and, blessing him, they departed.

Thus ends the story of Queen Humai, whose character, but for her one weakness, may be described as noble. In the *Avesta* she appears as "the holy Huma". She ruled over Iran for thirty-two years, and hers was the first reign of which we have historical knowledge. Among other things, she is credited with some ancient buildings in the neighbourhood of Persepolis in the Province Pars, whose ruins are still in existence.[1]

[1] For the original Persian text consult Vullers-Landauer, *Firdusii*, pp. 1755–74.

CHAPTER XII

NAHID

The story of Princess Nahid, or Olympias, of real history, though brief, should prove of vital interest, since she became the mother of no less a historic personage than Alexander the Great.

Darab, or Darius II, as he is generally known (425–405 B.C.), was, according to Firdausi's account, a mighty monarch. He invaded, we are told, the territory of Rum in the west, and defeated the Ruman army, which was led by the Kisra, whose name was Failakus, the Persian form of Philip. He was undoubtedly Philip of Macedon.

Failakus, weary of endless warfare with Iran, sent an envoy to Darab to discuss the question of his paying tribute. The Shah thereupon summoned his chiefs, and held consultation with them. Among other things, they told him of Princess Nahid, the Kisra's only daughter, and described her wondrous beauty. Darab's mind was, therefore, made up. Replying to the envoy, he stipulated that Failakus should send his daughter Nahid, together with the tribute, if he wished to save his honour and be left in peace. When the King of Rum received this message, he was exceedingly gratified at the idea of claiming the Shah of Iran as his own son-in-law, and hastened to make grand preparations for the event. Princess Nahid marched forth with a retinue of sixty damsels, each with a golden goblet in her hand filled with royal gems, and each wearing a golden crown and ear-rings. Thus King Failakus bestowed his daughter upon King Darab, and the beautiful Nahid became Queen of Iran.

Her happiness, however, proved short-lived. The Shah's love for her began to cool, and he gradually conceived a dislike for her till, finally, he sent her back to her father. Shortly afterwards, a son was born to her, named Sikander, or Alexander, and brought up by Failakus as his own son and heir. At the death of Failakus, Alexander succeeded to the throne of Rum.

So legend meets history; the proud Persians would not own that they had been vanquished by a foreigner, and they made the son of Philip of Macedon into the son of one of their own Kings. Darab had a son by name Dara. He is Darius III, or Darius Codomannus (337–330 B.C.). Firdausi narrates at length how Dara demanded the tribute from Alexander as promised by Philip, and how the people of Rum seized it as a pretext to invade Iran. Here the purely Iranian legend ends; the rest belongs to the legend of Alexander, which was composed at Alexandria in Egypt into the romance known as that of Pseudo-Callisthenes.[1]

[1] For the original Persian text consult Vullers-Landauer, *Firdusii*, pp. 1783–1804.

CHAPTER XIII

RUSHANAK

When Dara, or Darius III, King of Iran, lay dying after his third defeat by the Rumans, the news was brought to Sikander by two of the Shah's own ministers, who had stabbed him in the breast, thinking to gain favour with the Kisra. Sikander, overcome by rage and grief, ordered the treacherous pair to lead him to the spot where the King was lying, which they accordingly did. At the sight of Dara's death-like countenance and the blood upon his breast, Sikander wept with anguish and despair. Then, having set a guard over the two assassinators, he dismounted, and, taking the wounded monarch's head on his lap, chafed it tenderly, removing the heavy crown and unclasping the mail from his breast. He endeavoured to speak words of comfort and hope, but Dara knew his end was approaching, and prepared to meet it calmly, commending his soul to God. He besought Sikander to weep for him no more, but attend to his last request and fulfil the dearest wish of his heart. Sikander thereupon replied that he had but to command him. Dara then asked him to take his daughter Rushanak in marriage.

> "Thou mayst," he said, "see born to her a youthful prince,
> Who will revive the name of Asfandiyar,
> Relume the altar of Zarduhsht, take up
> The Zandavasta, heed the presages,
> The Feast of Sada and the Fanes of Fire,

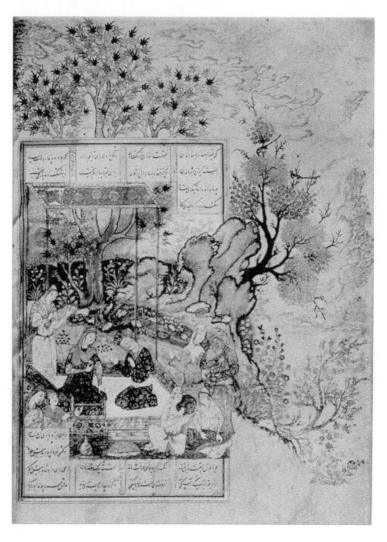

RUSHANAK IN THE PRESENCE OF ALEXANDER

(From a Persian Manuscript in the Metropolitan Museum of Art, New York

With glorious Nauruz, Urmuzd and Mihr,
And lave his soul and face in wisdom's stream,
Restore the customs of Luhrasp and follow
The doctrine of Gushtasp, maintain both high
And low in their degree, illume the Faith
And see good days."[1]

Sikander promised faithfully to carry out the Shah's wish. Dara extended his hand to grasp that of the other, then fell back dead.

The throne therefore passed to Sikander. Mindful of his pledge to Dara, he lost no time in bringing about its fulfilment. He summoned a scribe, and instructed him to indite a preliminary letter to Dilarai, the mother of Rushanak, also one to the Princess herself. Dilarai, on receiving her letter, mourned bitterly the death of her husband, and returned a grateful reply to Sikander; Rushanak also wrote, accepting his offer. Sikander then requested his mother, Nahid, to go to Dilarai's palace and see the Princess Rushanak, taking with her loads of gold brocade and tapestry, numberless gems, three hundred Ruman damsels and many more gifts. Nahid departed to do her son's bidding, and Dilarai came forward in royal array to meet her, amidst much pomp and rejoicing. Gorgeous wedding gear had been prepared for Rushanak, and, when she rode forth to meet the Shah, none had ever looked on such splendour.

They raised triumphal arches in the cities:
All lips were smiling, all hearts full.

[1] Warner, *The Shāhnāma*, vol. VI, p. 55.

And Sikander, beholding the Princess, her beauty, her sweet and modest mien, fell in love with her at sight, and forthwith made her his queen.

The arrangement made between King Dara and Alexander that the latter should marry Roxana, or Rushanak, appears in the Pseudo-Callisthenes, in all its versions, but is not historical. We have seen that, according to Firdausi, she was the daughter of Dara, or Darius III, but according to the earlier accounts, she was the daughter of Oxyartes, a Bactrian chief, whose stronghold Alexander escaladed. We are told, in these writings, that Alexander was enamoured of her at sight, and married her in the year 328 B.C.[1]

---

[1] For the original Persian text consult Macan, *The Shāhnāma*, pp. 1280–90.

THE ASHKANIAN PERIOD
From 330 B.C. *to* A.D. 225

CHAPTER XIV

GULNAR

Gulnar,[1] a beautiful and fascinating damsel, was a captive at the court of the Parthian King, Ardawan, at Rai.[2] The King loved her dearly, and was never so happy as when in her society. He gave her a palace to dwell in, and made her keeper of his treasury. One day she wandered out on to the balcony, and, gazing downwards, beheld in the vicinity of Ardawan's stables, a handsome youth with whom she fell in love at sight. Having ascertained his place of abode, she resolved to make known to him the state of her feelings at the first opportunity. Accordingly, when night fell she crept silently out and tied a lasso to the battlements, then descended boldly and went to seek the youth. He was sleeping when she entered, but she raised his head and clasped it to her, so that he awakened and gazed at her in wonder, imagining, from her beauteous face and form, that she must be a vision. When he, however, enquired whence she came, she replied that she was his slave and loved him heart and soul. She then informed him of her position at the court of Ardawan, adding that she would gladly relinquish all for his sake.

---

[1] The name means "Pomegranate-bloom".

[2] The ancient city of Ragha in the *Avesta*, the birthplace of Zoroaster's mother, according to tradition. Its ruined site can still be identified a few miles southward from Teheran.

The youth who had thus won the affections of Gulnar proved to be Ardshir, son of Papak, of the family of Sasan, the tribal King of Pars. From his childhood, Ardshir Papakan had displayed unusual intelligence, and given promise of marked ability as a warrior, so that, by the time he reached manhood his name was on many lips. In due course, King Ardawan came to hear of his prowess, and wrote to Papak, urging him to send the young hero into his presence. Papak, though unwilling to part with his son, could not but comply with the King's wish; also, he felt ambitious for the boy, Ardawan having promised to place him among the great chiefs of his court. He therefore sent Ardshir, richly attired, to Ardawan's palace, where the King received him royally, assigning him a place beside the throne, and treating him almost as a son. But this happy state of affairs came to an abrupt termination when the King, in company with his own four sons and Ardshir, was engaged in the chase one day. Ardshir, having pressed on in front of his companions, saw a wild ass, and, taking aim, brought it instantly to the ground. Ardawan seeing the shot was filled with admiration, and cried: "May he that shot possess a soul to match his hand!" Ardshir replied: "I shot the wild ass". A son said: "'Twas I who brought it down". This gave rise to a somewhat heated argument between the two young men, in which Ardshir appeared in the ascendancy. The King thereupon grew angry with him, and spoke bitter words, blaming himself for what he now considered misplaced kindness towards the youth, who in return was bent only on surpassing his sons. He then dismissed him curtly, ordering him to the stables, of which he should now be master. Ardshir departed in sorrow, and became keeper of the King's Arab steeds, choosing a lodging near at hand. He afterwards wrote to his father, telling him the whole story. Papak was much troubled on receiving the letter, and in his reply deplored the lad's foolish behaviour, and counselled him to act more wisely in future, remembering he was but the King's servant. He also sent a supply of gold, promising him more when that should be exhausted. Ardshir therefore procured for himself fine raiment, furnished his lodging accordingly and spent his time in feasting and revelry. But when, a short time later, Papak died, the youth was inconsolable. He brooded darkly on his hated position in Ardawan's service, and forthwith set himself to devise some means of escape.

Now to return to the story of Gulnar. One day King Ardawan brought to court some learned astrologers, and commanded them to read his horoscope. The wise men betook themselves to Gulnar's mansion, and spent three days in studying the stars, while Gulnar remained ever at hand, listening secretly to their discussions. When their observations were completed, she overheard them say that a chief of noble birth was destined to destroy Ardawan and subsequently become the monarch of Iran. As soon as it was dark, she hastened to Ardshir with this information, having in her mind that he might prove to be the noble chief. The youth's spirits rose at her words. He besought her to leave Ardawan and fly with him, vowing that a throne and crown should be hers, to which Gulnar answered: "Thy slave am I, and death alone shall part us". Then, having made plans to escape the following day, she hastened back to the palace, unlocked the treasury and took her choice of the royal gems. The next night, at the appointed hour, she went to meet Ardshir, who had all in readiness for their flight. A moment later, on Arab steeds, one grey and the other black, they rode forth in the direction of Pars.

When on the morrow the news reached the ears of Ardawan, he became wellnigh distracted at the thought of losing his beloved Gulnar, and lost no time in following the pair. On his way he made enquiries as to whether anyone had seen a man and woman pass mounted on a grey and a black steed, and was told that such a couple had ridden by, followed by a mountain sheep.[1] On hearing this, his ministers informed him that the sheep running behind the fugitives signified that the stars were in their favour. Meanwhile, Ardshir and Gulnar, hot and fatigued beyond measure, had paused by a stream, and were about to alight and slake their thirst. They were, however, warned against tarrying by two mysterious youths, who urged them to proceed with haste if they valued their lives. Such words, so earnestly spoken, could not be disregarded; so, gathering together all their remaining strength, they rushed on, with

[1] Compare Yasht 14. 23, where we are told that Verethraghna, the *Yazata* of Victory, goes forth in the form of a graceful ram.

RECITATION OF POEMS TO THE ACCOMPANIMENT OF MUSIC

(From a Persian Manuscript in the Metropolitan Museum of Art, New York)

Ardawan ever pursuing them. The King halted from place
to place to make enquiries, and heard again and again the
singular story of the mountain sheep. So significant did it
appear to his wise men that he was compelled to heed their
advice. They bade him abandon the pursuit and return to
Rai, there to prepare for war. And Ardawan, in deepest
dejection, obeyed.

In due course, what had been foretold came to pass.
Ardshir gathered an army, made war against Ardawan and
slew him, thus becoming King of Iran and founder of the
Sasanian dynasty in A.D. 226. He revived the Zoroastrian
religion, which had its beginning during the reign of Gushtasp, as we have seen. He also restored and collected the
Zoroastrian scriptures, which had been in a scattered state
after the invasion of Persia by Alexander and the downfall
of the Achaemenian Empire.[1]

[1] For the original Persian text consult Macan, *The Shāhnāma*, pp.
1365-79.

THE SASANIAN PERIOD
From A.D. 226 *to* A.D. 651

CHAPTER XV

DILAFRUZ-I-FARRUKHPAI

When Shapur (Sapor II, A.D. 309-379), son of Hurmuzd, had for some time occupied the throne of Iran, he began to feel some curiosity as to the Kisra of Rum, his army, treasury and general affairs of state. He therefore resolved to visit the country disguised as a merchant from Iran. Taking with him many camels loaded with costly wares, he journeyed into Rum and made his way to the Kisra's palace. Saluting the chamberlain, he bestowed upon him rich gifts and requested him to make his presence known to the King, who, he said, might take his choice from among his merchandise. His purpose, he explained, was but to seek protection while on business in Rum. The chamberlain departed with the message, and, a moment later, Shapur was admitted to the royal presence. The King received him cordially and invited him to partake of refreshments.

There was, however, among the Kisra's courtiers, a native of Iran, a man of no very lofty attributes, who, having noted the "merchant" secretly, his looks, speech and bearing, drew the King aside and asserted that he was none other than Shapur, the King of Kings. The Kisra was astounded; then he grew wrathful and determined the impostor should not escape. Therefore, as soon as Shapur arose from the table, his wits muddled with the quantity of wine he had taken, he was seized by the guard and carried away to the women's section of the palace. His hands were then bound and his body sewn up in an ass's skin. They finally cast the luckless monarch into a dark and gloomy cell, and gave instructions that he was to be fed on nought but bread and water. This, said the Kisra, would bring him a lingering death, and thus give him time to reflect upon all he had lost. He then led his forces into Iran, and returned to Rum victorious.

Meanwhile, Shapur, in his misery, had won the compassion of a beautiful damsel, who was slave to the Kisra's wife. All day long she thought of him with pity, and, whenever possible, contrived to visit him. On one of these occasions, she begged him to tell her his story, and he said he would do so on condition that she promised to keep it secret. She swore that she would never betray him, and he thereupon told her all. He further besought her to bring him warm milk at meal times, with which to soak the ass's hide, and thus render it supple. The kind-hearted girl, though ever fearful of discovery, performed this service faithfully, so that at the end of two weeks the hide had moistened sufficiently to allow Shapur to emerge therefrom. With aching body and full heart, he blessed the damsel, and vowed she should be exalted over all women and the world be at her feet. He then asked her aid in devising some means of escape, and she told him that a festival was to be held in Rum the next day, which all would attend. She promised, as soon as the Queen had departed, to have two steeds in readiness; the following night would then be their opportunity. Praising her courage and resource, Shapur returned to his solitary cell and eagerly looked forward to the morrow. The damsel proved as good as her word. Two splendid horses, some weapons and a goodly store of jewels were in waiting, and full of secret joy the couple rode forth to safety and Iran. On they sped, night and day, pausing neither for food nor rest, until at length, overcome with fatigue, they dismounted and sought hospitality at a gardener's cottage. The good man opened his eyes wide on beholding their armour, and inquired the meaning of such a visitation. Shapur told him that he was a traveller from Iran and in danger from the Kisra. He implored the man to be his host that night, assuring him that his kindness should one day be handsomely rewarded. The gardener immediately placed his house at the disposal of Shapur and his fair companion, and promised to inform no one of the circumstance. His wife prepared for them food and drink and quarters for the night. Passing wine to Shapur, the good man said: "Drink to whom thou wilt". And Shapur answered: "My host". But the excellent man insisted upon his guest taking the lead, saying:

> The man of Grace it behoveth first to drink;
> For verily a crown upon thy locks I scent.

Shapur smiled as he took the wine, and then asked for news of Iran. His host proceeded to recount the misfortunes of that unhappy land: its population scattered, its crops ruined, massacre and pillage rife.

"Where, then," enquired Shapur, "was the King?"
The gardener turned a tragic face upon him as he told of
the Shah's strange disappearance, adding that the people of
Iran were slaves in Rum. By this time, the worthy man was
more than a little suspicious as to the degree of nobility
borne by his guest, and pressed him to prolong his stay for
the space of three days. Thus, he thought, would his humble
abode gain fame for evermore. He was also hoping Shapur
might divulge his name when in his cups.

On the morning of his departure, Shapur requested his
host to fetch him some seal-clay. The man obeyed. Taking
the clay from him, the monarch pressed his signet upon it;
then returned it to him with instructions that he should bear
it to the high priest of Iran. The gardener went promptly
to do his bidding, but on his arrival found the portal barred,
and guarded by armed men. He clamoured loudly to be
admitted, and finally had his way. When the high priest saw
the impress on the clay, he became greatly excited, and put
many questions to the gardener concerning his guest's
appearance, manner and speech. Satisfied from the man's
answers that this could be none other than the Shah himself,
he immediately gave orders for troops to be assembled, and,
as night approached, soldiers gathered from every quarter
and made for the gardener's cottage. Shapur received them
joyously; then proceeded to tell them the tale of his sufferings, and of the slave-girl's heroism. He spoke of her in
terms of the highest praise, and vowed he was henceforth
her slave. Then, cautioning the troops to observe strict

secrecy, he began to make plans for an attack on Rum. And
so it came to pass that the Kisra was defeated, and men were
wont to allude to Shapur as "The Victorious Shah".

Shapur was Shah all his life, contemporary with ten
Roman Emperors, and was one of the greatest of Sasanian
rulers. And he never ceased to love and cherish the damsel
to whom he owed not only his greatness, but his life. He
bestowed on her the name *Dilāfruz-i-Farrukhpāi*, which
has the charming meaning, "Lucky-footed Lustre-of-the-
Heart".[1]

[1] For the original Persian text consult Macan, *The Shāhnāma*, pp.
1439-52.

CHAPTER XVI

SAPINUD

King Bahram Gur[1] (Varahran V, A.D. 420–438), son of Yazdagird, journeyed into Hindustan in the rôle of an envoy sent by the Shah to demand tribute from the Indian King, Shangul. The Hindu ruler received the disguised messenger with all honour, and he and his followers were greatly impressed by his valour and prowess. Among other deeds of daring, he slew a wolf and a dragon, and, in polo and other games, far surpassed the Indian players. All were astonished at his horsemanship, and the King of Hindustan began to fear that on his return to Iran the ambassador might inform the Shah as to the inferiority of the horsemen in Hindustan, in consequence of which the Iranian heroes would invade his country. He therefore resolved to kill Bahram; but his wise men intervened, warning him that Iran would most surely avenge his death After some consideration, King Shangul decided that it would be more diplomatic to create a bond of friendship between Iran and Hindustan; this he thought he might accomplish by bestowing upon the young warrior the hand of one of his three fair daughters. Calling Bahram, he spoke to him on the subject, and found him more than agreeable. He forthwith sent for the princesses that Bahram

[1] Familiar to the Occident as "the Great Hunter" through Fitzgerald's version of Omar Khayyam.

BAHRAM MARRIES SAPINUD

(From a Persian Manuscript in the Metropolitan Museum of Art, New York)

might choose from among them. His choice fell upon Sapinud, a slender, graceful beauty, possessed withal of much intelligence and sweetness of disposition. The wedding was celebrated shortly afterwards, with rejoicings that lasted the entire week.

One day, as the happy pair sat conversing lovingly together, Bahram let Sapinud into the secret of his identity. She turned on him eyes bright with wonder that she should be the bride of the illustrious Bahram Gur himself. Later, he told her that he wished to quit Hindustan secretly and return to Iran. He asked her whether she would consent and go with him, thus to be Queen and share his throne. Her answer was that of a loving wife, whose joy is but to serve her husband faithfully. With her characteristic woman's wit, she promptly set herself to frame a scheme by which they could escape. She informed him that, in five days' time, a festival was to be held at some distance from the city. As the King, her father, would attend the feast, together with all the soldiers in the city, they would take advantage of the opportunity and depart the same night. Bahram caught at the plan with enthusiasm, and all was arranged accordingly.

The day of the festival having arrived, Sapinud went to her father and told him her husband was indisposed, begging on that account to be excused attending the feast. The King sympathetically granted her request, then took his departure. When night came on, Bahram and Sapinud stole quietly from the palace. Seating his wife upon her palfrey,

Bahram invoked God's name over her in *Avesta*, or ancient
Persian. The couple then rode hastily to the river, evidently
the River Indus, where Bahram procured a skiff, into
which he tenderly helped Sapinud, then quickly pulled
off. They landed as the sun was just rising in the heavens.

When the news of their flight reached the ears of Shangul,
he instantly rode in pursuit, and overtook them by the
river. He upbraided his daughter and threatened to kill
her; then, turning to Bahram, accused him of double dealing
and ingratitude. Touched by his grief, Bahram Gur revealed himself as the King of Iran and Turan, and added
that the father of Sapinud should ever be honoured for his
goodness to him.

> "And thy child," he said, "shall be
> The Lustre of the West and Crown of Dames."

King Shangul bowed low and embraced his son-in-law,
the mighty monarch of Iran. Each asked pardon of the
other. Then Shangul took his farewell, and Bahram and
Sapinud rode on joyfully to the land of Iran, where they
were received with great pomp and splendour.

Some time afterwards they were visited by Shangul. He
clasped Sapinud to him and kissed her in deep affection,
and bestowed on her wondrous silks and gems. Before
returning to Hindustan, he drew up a deed of gift, be-
queathing the whole of his treasury—crown, kingdom,
throne and casque—to noble Bahram Gur. This he commanded to be written on silk, so we are told, and given
into the keeping of his daughter. Sapinud was in due

course received into the Zoroastrian religion, and became through her sweet, kindly nature a shining example of the faith.[1]

[1] For the original Persian text consult Macan, *The Shāhnāma*, pp. 1558-79.

CHAPTER XVII

GURDYA

We come to an interesting heroine, strong alike in love for her own country, and for a brother whose ambitious aims she sought in vain to direct in the path of loyalty to the Shah.

She is Gurdya, the sister of Bahram Chubina, chief captain in the City of Rai, who revolted against Hurmuzd (Hormisdas IV, A.D. 578–590), the son of Nushirwan and King of Iran, and strove to take possession of the throne. Bahram was exceedingly fond of Gurdya, of whom he had had charge ever since she had been left an orphan in her early childhood. He had the highest opinion of her character and intellect, and in consequence, made much of her.

One day, when he and a few of his chiefs were engaged in plotting against the King, Gurdya suddenly appeared from behind the curtain and addressed Bahram sternly:

"Design not evil, brother," she admonished him.
"Make not greed the lord over wisdom."

The chiefs could not but be impressed by her words and her earnestness; but Bahram strongly resented her advice, and sat brooding darkly until, with a show of indifference, he resumed the conversation with his confederates, and Gurdya left the scene in tears, bitterly disappointed in her brother.

Bahram began secretly to prepare for war. He first addressed a letter to King Hurmuzd, stating that he refused to accept him as King, and that Khusrau Parwiz should be the ruler. He privately gave orders for new coins to be issued, bearing the superscription of Khusrau Parwiz. In this way, he poisoned the mind of Hurmuzd against his own son, so that the monarch planned to put Parwiz to death. The young Prince, however, managed to escape from Iran. Soon after this, the King's own brothers, who had been imprisoned for some time, sought him out and as an act of revenge blinded him. Khusrau Parwiz then returned to Iran, as the people wished to make him King. On beholding his father's terrible affliction, his heart was touched, and he instantly forgave him all. The throne duly passed to him.[1]

The rebellious Bahram now rose against Khusrau, and the shrewd Gurdya, becoming aware of his designs, once more warned him against stirring up strife. The King, she pointed out, was young and hot-headed, and, on that account, was it not better to let well alone? This time her brother paid heed to her counsels, acknowledging that she spoke truly. But he told her regretfully that it was now too late to draw back; hostilities were already in progress.

Khusrau Parwiz fled to Rum, where he enlisted the sympathy of the Emperor, who placed an army at his disposal that he might succeed in overthrowing Bahram Chubina. With these forces, Khusrau once more entered

[1] Khusrau Parwiz (Chosroes II, A.D. 590–628), was contemporary with three Eastern Roman Emperors: Maurice (A.D. 582–602), Phocas (A.D. 602–610), and Heraclius (A.D. 610–642).

Iran. Twice he was defeated by Bahram, but the third time
he was victorious, and Bahram lay mortally wounded.

When the news was brought to Gurdya, she hastened to
her brother's side. In an agony of grief, she knelt down and
lifting his head on to her lap smoothed back the hair from
his damp brow, and endeavoured to soothe him. And
Bahram drew her face down to his and kissed her again and
again, and spoke many loving words of appreciation of her
loyalty and wisdom. A few moments later he died and
Gurdya turned away, plunged in the deepest sorrow and
despair. She had a silver coffin made for him, and, wrapping
his warrior form in brocade, laid her beloved brother to
rest.

Immediately afterwards a messenger appeared, bearing a
letter to Gurdya from the Khan of Chin (China, or Chinese
Turkistan), asking her hand in marriage. Gurdya sent back
a reply, saying that such a proposal was ill-timed; in four
months' time, however, she would consider it. She then
sought her counsellors, to whom she reported the circumstance, laying indignant emphasis on the Khan's having
waited until her brother's death before making the offer.
She began to unfold a plan by which to escape from Marv
into Iran. Her counsellors listened wonderingly, and
declared themselves her slaves. The valiant maiden then
went forth to inspect the troops, selecting from among their
number eleven hundred and three score, each one of whom
would readily face ten cavaliers. She next donned her
brother's suit of armour and, reappearing before her forces,

delivered an address, concluding with the words: "All that
disapprove, abide ye here!" One and all shouted: "We
are lieges and obey". Then, like some illustrious cavalier,
Gurdya sprang upon her brother's charger, and, swift as
the wind, led the host upon its way.

Through the treachery of a few deserters, however, news
of her flight came to the ears of the Khan. He became very
angry, and promptly despatched an army of six thousand in
pursuit of her, under the leadership of his chief, Tuwurg.
He gave particular instructions that no hostility should be
shown unless resistance were offered. Tuwurg, with his
troops, departed and overtook Gurdya and her doughty
band within four days. In her armour, he failed to recognise
the fair lady whom he sought, and thereupon began to
make enquiries for Gurdya. She came boldly forward and
said that she was Gurdya. Tuwurg was greatly taken aback,
but, recovering himself, gave her the Khan's message, which
ran to the effect that, if she did not consent to become his
wife, she was to be taken prisoner. These imperious words
but roused wondrous spirit in Gurdya. She instantly flung
forth a challenge to Tuwurg and spurring forward her
steed slew the chief and a great number of his army. She
then despatched a messenger to King Khusrau with the information that she had defeated the army of the Khan of Chin.

Meanwhile, Gustaham (Bistam, Vistakhma), maternal
uncle of Khusrau Parwiz, who had effected the murder of
King Hurmuzd and still staunchly supported the lost cause
of Bahram Chubina, began to fear that Khusrau might put

him to death as a traitor. Hearing about Gurdya, he fled
to her for refuge. Then, seeking the general of her army,
he entreated him to plead with her on his behalf, as he
desired to wed her. The general went to Gurdya and said
much in praise of Gustaham, dwelling on his devotion to
her brother, which the sagacious warrior knew to be a sure
way to her heart. In due course she was persuaded into
marrying him. She could not know that Gustaham's chief
purpose was to join her forces in the overthrow of King
Khusrau. Shortly afterwards, Gustaham's fears were
realised; he was seized and assassinated one night, at the
King's instigation. Khusrau then sent a message to Gurdya,
asking her to be his queen. She forthwith presented herself
to him in all her beauty and valour, and the King remembering the great loyalty with which she had ever served
him, fell in love with her instantly, and married her.

One day, at Khusrau's request, she gave an exhibition of
her prowess. All were astounded at her bravery. She was
at once appointed overseer of the royal bower.

It happened that about this time the people of Rai were
much oppressed, owing to the harshness of their ruler.
Gurdya went to the King and asked him to grant the city
to her command as a fief, because of her special interest in
that province. The King immediately fulfilled her desire,
when she not only relieved the people from distress, but
saved the capital City of Rai.[1]

[1] For the original Persian text consult Macan, *The Shāhnāma*, pp.
1851–1989.

CHAPTER XVIII

SHIRIN

Shirin was a Princess, whose name is handed down to lasting fame in all later Persian romantic literature. According to Firdausi, she was of Persian descent and came from Khuzistan. She became the consort of the famous Sasanian monarch, Khusrau Parwiz, and the poets never tire of recounting the King's devotion to her.

Khusrau Parwiz first fell in love with the beautiful Shirin during the lifetime of his father, King Hurmuzd. As narrated in the previous chapter, when Hurmuzd was deposed, Bahram Chubina raised a rebellion, and Khusrau had perforce to devote himself to the war against the would-be contestant for the crown. After a severe struggle, Bahram was compelled to seek refuge with the Khan of Chin. Meanwhile, Shirin wept in solitude that Prince Khusrau, in order to support his royal father's interests should thus neglect her. Khusrau returned victorious and shortly afterwards succeeded to the throne.

One day, while hunting with several other Princes and Knights, Khusrau chanced to draw nigh to the palace where Shirin dwelt. Hearing news of this, she donned a beautiful gown of red brocade of Rum and bedecking herself with rich jewels, placed a royal crown upon her head. She then made her way out on to the terrace, and, when

Khusrau Parwiz appeared in sight, addressed him in the
following sorrowful words:

> O Shah! Great Lion!
> O framed to be leader of the host!
> O blessed hero lion-conqueror!
> Where is that love of thine? Where are the tears
> Of blood once staunched by looking on Shirin?
> Where all those days which once we turned to nights,
> Tears in our hearts and eyes, smiles on our lips?
> Where are our loves, our troth, our bonds, our oaths?[1]

Khusrau, hearing her, became stricken with remorse at
having so neglected his beloved. In the care of his most
trusted chieftains, he sent Shirin to his golden bower, and,
as soon as the chase was over, returned to the palace to
marry her. The nobles heard these tidings and advised
Khusrau against taking her as his Queen; but the Shah
defended the lady, assuring his loyal retainers that she had
ever been true to him. The nobles were therefore satisfied,
and gave their assent. It happened that King Khusrau had
still another wife, a daughter of the Kisra of Rum, named
Maryam. She was a wise and beautiful Princess, and Khusrau Parwiz was very fond of her, and had made her the
chief Queen in the royal bower. After her death, however,
which occurred shortly after the King's marriage to Shirin,
the latter succeeded her in the golden chambers, and took
her place as the chief Queen.

It may here be observed that Firdausi entirely omits the
tragical episode of Shirin and her sculptor-lover Farhad.

---

[1] Warner, *The Shāhnāma*, vol. VIII, p. 385.

KHUSRAU ARRIVES AT SHIRIN'S PALACE

(From a Persian Manuscript in the Metropolitan Museum of Art, New York)

This doubtlessly true story is, however, given by Nizami in
his romantic poem of *Khusrau and Shīrīn*, and may here be
appropriately recounted, in order to complete the story of
one of the most fascinating personalities of Ancient Iran.
The following is the tale as told by Nizami.

Khusrau Parwiz became jealous of Farhad, the renowned
sculptor, who carved in stone imperishable records of the
King's fame, but who had fallen in love with Shirin. To
encourage the work of the artist's chisel, Khusrau promised
him the favours of the fair Shirin. Unceasingly the sculptor
toiled, and wrought miracles in the living rock, which are
still to be seen. But when the achievement was almost
accomplished, the monarch sought for some means to
postpone the fulfilment of his promise. He therefore called
his courtiers to him, and asked their advice as to how he
might rid himself of this rival. The courtiers suggested that
he should appoint Farhad some task that would occupy him
throughout the whole of his life. Now, Shirin had asked of
Khusrau a "river of milk". Khusrau, recalling this, summoned Farhad into his presence, and bade him hew a
passage through the great mountain Bahistun, so as to join
the rivers on the opposite sides. Farhad, the true love,
replied that he would accomplish this upon one condition:
namely, that the fair Shirin be given to him as the reward
for his labour. As Khusrau Parwiz was certain that the
work would never be finished since it would surely require
superhuman power, he consented. The sculptor then began
his work, thinking but of Shirin all the while. He toiled

without pause on the mountain, described by Nizami
thus:

> The mist of night around her summit coils,
> But still Farhad, the lover-artist, toils,
> And still—the flashes of his axe between—
> He sighs to ev'ry wind, Alas! Shirin!
> Alas! Shirin!—my task is well nigh done.
> The goal in view for which I strive alone.
> Love grants me power that Nature might deny;
> And whatsoe'er my doom, the world shall tell,
> Thy lover gave to immortality
> Her name he loved—so fatally—so well![1]

The poor sculptor continued his work, ever hopeful of
winning Shirin, and completed it within a short time. In
the front of the arch he constructed the statue of Shirin
surrounded by attendants like a queen, and in the middle
he carved in high relief the statue of Khusrau Parwiz seated
upon his favourite horse, Shabdiz, and panoplied in armour.
Under this arch, which is called Taq-i-Bustan[2] the rivers
were made to flow on either side, as Khusrau had commanded, and the chance traveller can still gaze in wonder-
ment upon the triumphs wrought by the sculptor-lover's
chisel.[3]

The romantic artist's end was tragic. When Farhad's
wonderful work was complete, Khusrau was much distressed. He was advised by his courtiers to bring about the
death of Farhad. Accordingly, one day, while the sculptor

[1] See Louisa Costello, *Rose Garden of Persia*, p. 92.
[2] Situated in western Persia, near Kirmanshah of to-day.
[3] See especially Jackson, *Persia Past and Present*, New York, 1911,
pp. 213–28.

was at work high upon the rocky precipice, he sent an old woman to tell him that Shirin was dead. In a croaking voice she called aloft to him that he had now best prepare a tomb for her. The true lover, when he heard this news, raised a cry to Heaven: "Alas, Shirin!" flung from him chisel and mallet, and sprang from the towering cliff, to perish at its base. When Shirin learned of the fate of her artist-lover, she wept tears of bitter sorrow.

We shall turn once more to Firdausi's narrative of Khusrau and Shirin. Maryam had left a son, named Shirwi, also known as Kubad. Now, Khusrau Parwiz knew that Shirwi was not worthy of the crown or throne, so he put him in prison, in comfortable quarters. He was, however, later released by some of his chiefs, and rose in arms against his father, with the help of his grandfather, the Kisra of Rum, and succeeded in overpowering and taking him prisoner. Shirin was devoted to Khusrau and shared his grief in captivity. The life of Khusrau Parwiz was finally demanded by his enemies, whereupon his treacherous son Shirwi, a timid man, hired an assassin to kill him. When this was brought to pass, Shirwi actually wept and mourned his father. Such, according to the *Shāhnāma*, was the end of Khusrau, the mighty monarch of Iran.

After the death of King Khusrau, Shirwi came to the throne, and when two months had passed, he sent for Shirin. She returned the answer that she would come into his presence if the wise men of his court were also assembled for the occasion. Shirwi accordingly summoned all the

soothsayers, and Shirin thereupon entered the new royal
presence, unveiled her face and spoke thus:

> There is my face,
> Such as it is. If there be falsehood show it.
> My hair was all my hidden excellence,
> For none on earth e'er used to look thereon.
> What I display is all my sorcery,
> Not necromancy, fraud, and evil bent.[1]

Shirwi was quite dazzled at the sight of her lovely face, and
promptly asked her to be his Queen. Shirin replied that
she would consent, provided he would assign to her all her
treasure. Shirwi acceded to her request, and Shirin forthwith distributed her wealth to the poor, at the same time
freeing all her slaves. She then told Shirwi that she had one
more request to make: this was to have the charnel house
of Khusrau Parwiz opened that she might look upon her
dear lord's face again. Shirwi instantly granted this wish.
Whereupon Shirin went, weeping and wailing in anguish,
to the tomb, took poison on the spot, and dropped dead
by the side of her deceased husband.

Concerning Khusrau's own genuine love for Shirin there
can be no real historic ground for doubt. Fiction is borne
out by fact. In support of this statement may be cited that
a later Persian writer definitely records that, at *Kasr-i-Shīrīn*,
"Palace of Shirin", in the region of Khanikin,[2] there was
to be seen on the palace portal an inscription,[3] which was

---

[1] Warner, *The Shāhnāma*, vol. IX, p. 39.
[2] Situated in western Persia.
[3] Now lost, but possibly to be some day recovered.

SHIRIN GOES TO SEE THE ROCK-CARVINGS BY FARHAI

(From a Persian Manuscript in the Metropolitan Museum of Art, New York)

prepared by King Khusrau Parwiz. The rhyming couplet
ran as follows:

huzhīrā, ba-gaihān anūshah bi-zī
jihān rā ba-dīdār tōshah barī

TO THE FAIR SHIRIN

Ah, Beauteous One! Upon this earth, happy for aye do live!
Since to the world by thy mere glance such joyance thou dost give.[1]

Shirin is the only woman of the heroic past whose statue
is still preserved in Persia, if we are to believe an anonymous
Persian poet of more than a thousand years ago, who
identified the figures in the sculptured arch of Taq-i-Bustan
as Khusrau, Shirin and the high priest of the Magi.[2] But
some modern scholars are inclined to interpret these bas-
reliefs differently. In any event, Shirin stands out for all
time as one of the most romantic characters in the *Shāhnāma*
of Firdausi and in later Persian poetry.[3]

[1] See Jackson, *Early Persian Poetry*, p. 11.
[2] See Jackson, *Persia Past and Present*, p. 225.
[3] For the original Persian text consult Macan, *The Shāhnāma*, pp.
1998–2004, 2043–2050.

CHAPTER XIX

PURANDUKHT

After the death of Shirwi (A.D. 628), who ruled only for seven months, several other of the sons of Khusrau Parwiz ruled over Iran; but all were murdered by different conspirators, until no Princes were left. Thus, for a considerable period, the country had no King. Eventually, however, the people gave the throne and crown to Princess Purandukht, a sister of Shirwi, and a descendant of Sasan.

Purandukht (Puranducht, A.D. 630–631) was a good and gentle lady, and had been horrified at the part Shirwi had taken to bring about his father's death. Now that the country had made her its Queen, she determined to purify the atmosphere, and to see that justice was adequately meted out to the wrongdoers and that peace prevailed. Her words, as she took her seat upon the throne, may serve as evidence of her great zeal:

> I will not have
> The people scattered and I will enrich
> The poor with treasure that they may not bide
> In their distress. God grant that in the world
> There may be none aggrieved, because his pain
> Is my calamity. I will expel
> Foes from the realm and walk in royal ways.[1]

Wise as she was good, Queen Purandukht very soon succeeded in reviving law and order in the land of Iran. But her reign proved all to brief. Within six months of her accession to the throne, she fell ill and died. Reflecting

[1] Warner, *The Shāhnāma*, vol. IX, p. 57.

on the sudden death of Purandukht, the poet gives us some of the finest couplets in the *Shāhnāma*, the wise man of Tus anticipating by many centuries some of the famous quatrains in the *Rubaiyat* of Omar Khayyam:

> Such is the process of the turning sky,
> So potent while so impotent are we!
> If thine be opulence or poverty,
> If life affordeth gain or loss to thee,
> If thou shalt win what thou desirest so,
> Or disappointed be in wretchedness,
> And whether thou be one of wealth or woe,
> Both woe and wealth will pass away no less.
> Reign as a Shah a thousand years, five score,
> For sixty years or thirty, ten or four,
> It cometh to one thing, when all is done,
> If thou hadst many years or barely one.
> Oh! may thine actions thine own comrades be,
> For they in every place will succour thee.
> Let go thy clutch upon this Wayside Inn
> Because a goodlier place is thine to win.
> If thine endeavour be to learning given,
> Thou wilt by knowledge roam revolving heaven.[1]

Purandukht was the first historical Shahbanu, who as reigning sovereign of Iran graced the throne of Cyrus and Darius, Ardshir and Shapur. Among other things, she is said to have restored the "True Cross", but it seems more probable that this was done in the reign of Ardshir, her predecessor on the throne of Iran, if the date of its elevation at Jerusalem—fourteenth of September in the year 629 of the Christian era—be correct.[2]

[1] Warner, *The Shāhnāma*, vol. IX, p. 58.

[2] For the original Persian text consult Macan, *The Shāhnāma*, pp. 2057, 2058.

CHAPTER XX

AZARMDUKHT

After the death of Purandukht, her sister Azarmdukht (Azermidocht, A.D. 631–632) came to the throne. Although a capable ruler, with excellent intentions, she seems to have been a somewhat formidable lady, intolerant and over-conscious of her power, as may be gathered from her first address to the people:

> O sages, veterans
> And masters of affairs! be just in all,
> And follow precedent, for ye hereafter
> Must make the bricks your pillow. I will foster
> The loyal liege, assist him with dinars
> And if he erreth be long suffering;
> But him that is disloyal and deserteth
> The way of wisdom and of precedent
> Will I suspend in shame upon the gibbet,
> Be he an Arab, Ruman cavalier,
> Or Persian Thane.[1]

We are told that the chief noble of the time, who was governor of Khurasan, wished to make Azarmdukht his wife, upon which she had him privately executed for his presumption. This noble's son was the Rustam, who fought valiantly against the Arabs and fell at the battle of Kadisiya some years later. On hearing of his father's fate Rustam, who was in temporary authority in Khurasan, marched with a great army against Azarmdukht, overthrew her and

[1] Warner, *The Shāhnāma*, vol. IX, p. 59.

put her to death. This occurred when the unfortunate
Queen had reigned but four months.

Azarmdukht was the last Persian Princess who ruled the
country of Iran in ancient times, and the last heroine whose
story is told in the *Shāhnāma*. Firdausi closes his poem with
the reign of Yazdagird (Isdegird III, A.D. 632–652), the
last of the Zoroastrian Emperors of Iran.[1]

---

[1] For the original Persian text consult Macan, *The Shāhnāma*,
pp. 2058, 2059.

EPILOGUE

CHAPTER XXI

EPILOGUE

Firdausi's heroines as depicted in his great epic, the *Shāhnāma*, have left us with several definite impressions. It is unquestionable that women have played an important part in Persia's history, and it is surprising to find that feminine freedom of speech and manner is by no means so modern as is generally supposed, but existed considerably over a thousand years ago. The characters described may not have played an important political rôle, although we find Gurdya influencing her brother's councils to a certain extent, and Humai and Purandukht ruling as sovereigns wisely and well. We find, too, examples of women not content to remain passive spectators in the armed struggles and rebellions which surrounded them, but taking active part in the hostilities, where they acquit themselves so worthily, that on their true identities being discovered their adversaries are amazed at their prowess.

Love is a predominant note running through all old romances, and it appears to be a very usual thing for Firdausi's heroes and heroines to be mutually attracted at first sight. There is nothing, however, which appeals more to human nature than mother-love, and in this Faranak stands out as a very noble example, for what could be more admirable than the self-sacrificing manner in which she gives

up all to save her child, and suffers the utmost privations
and distress on his account.

There is no need to dwell on the poet's descriptions of his
various heroines. Great beauty is always a quality possessed
by epic heroines, and those of Firdausi are no exception to
this rule. But while there may be a marked similarity in the
general appearance of his characters, each story is different
and individual, and the reader does not retain an impression
of constant repetition. On the contrary it is felt that here is
a very distinct group of persons, each with her own personality and her own ultimate fate, with the power to con-
trol her own destiny and that of her family and associates.
We have, in short, a picture of a highly civilised and
organised society.

It is the emphasis on the individuality of the heroines
that sets the work of Firdausi apart from other epic tales.
Homer and Virgil, with very few exceptions, portrayed a
man's world in which the women played at best a subor-
dinate rôle. Firdausi leads us into a society where women
are not mere shadows or reflections, but proud and strong
personalities, exerting considerable influence in the world of
their day. These living portraits of the heroines of ancient
Iran are worthy of admiration throughout the ages, and
the name of Firdausi lives on as one of the greatest bards
that the world has produced.

BIBLIOGRAPHY

A. WORKS OF REFERENCE

BARTHOLOMAE, CHRISTIAN. *Die Frau im sasanidischen Recht.* Heidelberg, 1924.

BROWNE, E. G. *A Literary History of Persia.* 4 vols. London, 1902–24.

COSTELLO, LOUISA. *The Rose Garden of Persia.* London, 1899.

DARMESTETER, JAMES. *Les Origines de la poésie persane.* Paris, 1887.

ETHÉ, HERMANN. *Die höfische und romantische Poesie der Perser.* Hamburg, 1887.

FIRDAUSI. *Firdusii Liber Regum qui inscribitur Schahname.* Edited by J. A. Vullers (and S. Landauer). 3 vols. Leyden, 1877–84.

—— Turner Macan's edition of the *Shāhnāma.* Calcutta, 1829.

—— *Le Livre des rois.* Traduit et commenté par Jules Mohl. 7 vols. Paris, 1876–78.

—— *Il Libro dei re, poema epico.* Recato dal persiano in versi italiani da Italo Pizzi. 8 vols. Turin, 1886–88.

—— *The Sháhnáma of Firdausí.* Done into English by Arthur George Warner and Edmond Warner. 9 vols. London, 1905–25.

—— *The Sháh Námah.* Translated and abridged in prose and verse by J. Atkinson. Edited by J. A. Atkinson. London, 1886. (Chandos Classics.)

—— *Firdosi's Königsbuch (Schahname).* Übersetzt von Friedrich Rückert, aus dem Nachlass herausgegeben von E. A. Bayer. 3 vols. Berlin, 1890, 1894, 1895. (Incomplete.)

—— *The Shah-namah.* Translated by Alexander Rogers. London, 1907. (Incomplete.)

JACKSON, A. V. WILLIAMS. *Early Persian Poetry.* New York, 1920.

JUSTI, FERDINAND. *Iranisches Namenbuch.* Marburg, 1895.

MIRKHOND. *History of the Early Kings of Persia.* Translated, from the original Persian, by David Shea. London, 1832.

NÖLDEKE, THEODOR. "Das iranische Nationalepos." In *Grundriss der iranischen Philologie*, vol. II, pp. 130–211. Strassburg, 1896–1904. (English translation by L. Bogdanov, in the *Journal of the K. R. Cama Oriental Institute*, no. 6, pp. 1–161. Bombay, 1925.)

RICE, O. C. *Persian Women and their Ways.* London, 1923.

ZIMMERN, HELEN. *The Epic of Kings, Stories retold from Firdusi.* London, 1882.

B. THE HEROINES OF HISTORY

CLAYTON, E. C. *Female Warriors. Memorials of Female Valour and Heroism, from the Mythological Ages to the Present Era.* 2 vols. London, 1879.

GLOVER, (Lady) J. S. *Great Queens. Famous Women Rulers of the East.* London, 1928.

GOODRICH, F. B. *Women of Beauty and Heroism, from Semiramis to Eugenie.* New York, 1859.

HAYS, (Mrs) MARY. *Female Biography; or, Memoirs of Illustrious and Celebrated Women, of all Ages and Countries.* 3 vols. Philadelphia, 1807.

JENKINS, J. S. *The Heroines of History.* New Orleans, 1854.

OWEN, (Mrs) O. F. *The Heroines of History.* New York, 1854.

POLLARD, E. B. *Women in all Ages and in all Countries.* 10 vols. Philadelphia, 1907–8.

REICH, EMIL. *Women through the Ages.* 2 vols. London, 1908.

STURGES, BEATRICE. *Beautiful Women of the Poets.* New York, 1897.

INDEX

Abtin, husband of Faranak, 5, 6, 11; called *Āthwya* in the *Avesta*, 5 n.
Achaemenian Empire, 71
Achaemenian period, 2, 40 n.
Afrasiyab, ruler of Turan, 25, 31–3, 35–7, 40
Ahran, Ruman chief, 46, 47
Alburz, mountain range, 7 and n., 14, 18; *Harā Berezaitī* in the *Avesta*, 7 n.
Alexander the Great, *see* Sikander
Alexandria in Egypt, 61
Arab geographies, 54 n. 2
Ardawan, King of Parthia, 67–71
Ardshir, son of Papak, 67–71, 97
Ardvi Sura Anahita, Goddess of Waters, 10
Arjasp, King of Turan called Arejataspa in the *Avesta*, 48, 49, 51, 52
Arnawaz, wife of Faridun, 10, 13, 52; called Arenavach in the *Avesta*, 10; Darmesteter's Erenavāc, 10 n.
Artaxerxes Longimanus, 53 n. 2
Asfandiyar, son of Gushtasp, 48–50, 52, 62; assumes name of Kharrad, 50
Ashkanian period, 2; stories of, 65–71
Asia Minor, *see* Rum
Athenaeus, story from, 44 n.
Athwyani clan, 5 n.
Avesta, or *Zandavasta*, or *Sacred Book of the Parsis*, 5 n., 10 and n., 42 and n. 2, 55, 62, 71
Azarmdukht or Azermidocht, sister of Purandukht and Queen of Iran, 98, 99
Azhi Dahaka, *see* Zahhak

Babylon, 5, 12
Baghdad, 11
Bahistun, mountain, 91
Bahman, King, called *Vohūman Ardashīr Dīrāzdast* in the Pahlavi writings, 53 and n., 54, 57, 59
Bahram Chubina, 84–7, 89
Bahram Gur, or Varahran V, King of Iran, 80–2; "the Great Hunter" in FitzGerald's Omar Khayyam, 80 n.
Balkh, 41 n.
Bih Afrid, daughter of Gushtasp and Katayun, 49, 50
Birmaya, or Purmaya, the famous cow, 6, 7, 11
Bishutan, son of Gushtasp, 48
Bistun, Mount, 40, (Bisitun, Behistun, *Bagistāna*) 40 n.
Bizhan, husband of Manizha, 35–41, 52

Chares of Mitylene, quotes Athenaeus, 44 n.
Chin (China, or Chinese Turkistan), Khan of, 86, 87, 89
China, *see* Chin
Costello, *Rose Garden of Persia*, 92 n. 1
Cyrus, 97

Dakiki, first conceives idea of turning the *Khvatāi-nāmak* into verse, 1
Dara, or Darius III, or Darius Codomannus, 61–4
Darab, or Darius II, son of Bahman and Humai, 55 and n., 56–61
Darius I, 97

Darius II, *see* Darab

Darius III, or Darius Codomannus, *see* Dara

Darmesteter, *Études Iraniennes*, 10 n.

Dijla, River, 11

Dilafruz-i-Farrukhpai, wife of Shapur, 76, 77, 79

Dilanjam, daughter of the Kisra of Rum, 45

Dilarai, mother of Rushanak, 63

Euphrates, the, called the *Farāt* in the Arab geographies, 54 n. 2

Failakus, or Philip of Macedon, 60, 61

Faranak, wife of Abtin and mother of Faridun, 5–9, 103

Farangis, daughter of Afrasiyab and wife of Siyawush, 31–4

Farat, River, 54 and n. 2

Farhad, sculptor and lover of Shirin, 90–2

Fariburz, son of Kai Kaus and husband of Farangis, 34

Faridun, son of Abtin and Faranak, husband of Shahrinaz and Arnawaz, 5–8, 10–13, 42, 52

Farukhzad, *see* Gushtasp

Firdausi, author of the *Shāhnāma*, or *Book of Kings*, 1, 2, 42 n. 2, 54 n. 2, 60, 61, 64, 89, 91, 93, 97, 99, 103, 104

FitzGerald's Omar Khayyam, 80 n.

Garsiwaz, brother of Afrasiyab, 32

Gazhdaham, father of Gurdafrid, 28, 29

Gazing-cup, Kai Khusrau's, 37

Giv, 34, 37

Gulnar, wife of Ardshir, 67–70

Gurdafrid, daughter of Gazhdaham, 28–30

Gurdya, sister of Bahram Chubina, 84–8, 103

Gurgin, 35, 37, 40

Gushtasp, son of Luhrasp, 42–9, 63; called Kava Vishtaspa in the *Avesta*, 42 and n. 2; assumes name of Farukhzad, 44

Gustaham, or Bistam, or Vistakhma, 87, 88

Hajir, castellan of the White Castle, 28

Helen of Troy, 52

Heraclius, Eastern Roman Emperor, 85 n.

Hindustan, 12, 80, 82

Homer, 104

Hormisdas IV, *see* Hurmuzd

Humai, daughter of Gushtasp and Katayun, wife of King Bahman, 49, 50, 53, 54, 56, 58, 59, 103; also known as *Cihrāzād*, 53 n.; called "the holy Huma" in the *Avesta*, 59

Hurmuzd, father of Shapur, 75

Hurmuzd, or Hormisdas IV, King of Iran, father of Khusrau Parwiz, 84, 85, 87, 89

Hutaosa, wife of Vishtaspa (Gushtasp), in the *Avesta*, 42 n. 2

Indus, River, 82

Iraj, son of Faridun and Arnawaz, 13

Iran, 13, 19, 25, 31, 32, 34–6, 38, 40, 42, 45, 47–50, 52, 53, 56, 58–62, 69, 75, 77, 78, 80–2, 86, 91, 93, 96, 97, 99, 104

Irman, territory, 35

Jackson, Professor A. V. Williams, 15 n., 17 n.; *Early Persian Poetry*, 26 n., 44 n., 95 n. 1; *Zoroaster*, 53 n. 2; *Persia Past and Present*, 92 n. 3, 95 n. 2

Jamasp, vizier to Gushtasp, 49, 50

Jamshid, King of Iran, 5, 10

Jerusalem, 97

Kabul, 14, 19
Kadisiya, battle of, 98
Kai Kaus, King of Iran, 24, 25, 31, 34
Kai Khusrau, son of Siyawush and Farangis, and King of Iran, 34, 35, 37, 38, 40–2
Kaianian period, 1; stories of, 21–64
Kasr-i-Shīrīn, "Palace of Shirin", 94
Katayun (Kitabun, Nahid), daughter of the Kisra of Rum and wife of Gushtasp, 42 and n. 2, 43–9
Kawa, a blacksmith, 8, 11
Khanikin, 94
Khusrau Parwiz, or Chosroes II, son of Hurmuzd and King of Iran, 85 and n., 87–96
Khuzistan, 89
Khvatāi-nāmak, or *Book of Sovereigns*, 1
Kirmanshah, 40 n., 92 n. 2

Le Strange, Guy, *The Lands of the Eastern Caliphate*, 23 n.
Luhrasp, father of Gushtasp and King of Iran, 42, 43, 47, 48, 63

Macan, *The Shāhnāma*, 64 n., 71 n., 79 n., 83 n., 88 n., 95 n. 3, 97 n. 2, 99 n.
Mahābhārata, 45 n.
Manizha, daughter of Afrasiyab, wife of Bizhan, 35–41, 52
Marv, 86
Maryam, daughter of Kisra of Rum and wife of Khusrau Parwiz, 90, 93
Maurice, Eastern Roman Emperor, 85 n.
Median period, 2
Mihrab, King of Kabul, 14, 18
Minuchihr, King of Iran, 17, 19
Mirin, Ruman chief, 45–7

Mirkhond, *History*, 42 n. 2
Mohl, *Le Livre des Rois*, 7 n.

Nahid, or Olympias, Princess, daughter of Failakus, wife of Darab, 60, 61, 63
Naotaras, noble house of, 42 n. 2
Nizami, author of *Khusrau and Shīrīn*, 91
Nushirwan, father of Hurmuzd, 84

Odatis, in Athenaeus, 44 n.
Olympias, *see* Nahid
Omar Khayyam, FitzGerald's, 80 n.; *Rubaiyat*, 97
Ormazd, god of the Persians, 9
Oxyartes, Bactrian chief, 64

Pahlavi writings, the, 42 n. 2, 53 n. 2
Papak, King of Pars, 68, 69
Pars, province, 59, 68, 70
Parthian period, 2
Parysatis, 53 n. 2
Persepolis, 59
Persian empire, 54 n. 2
Philip of Macedon, *see* Failakus
Phocas, Eastern Roman Emperor, 85 n.
Piran, statesman in Afrasiyab's court, 31, 33, 36, 38
Pishdadian period, 1; stories of, 3–19
Pseudo-Callisthenes, romance of, 61, 64
Purandukht, or Puranducht, sister of Shirwi and Queen of Iran, 96–8, 103

Ragha, birthplace of Zoroaster's mother, 67 n. 2
Rakhsh, favourite horse of Rustam, 23, 24, 39, 40
Rai, 67, 71, 84, 88
Rama, 52
Rāmāyana, Indian epic, 52

Rashnavad, general of Queen Humai, 56–8
Ravana, 52
Roxana, see Rushanak
Rudaba, daughter of Mihrab, wife of Zal and mother of Rustam, 14–19, 23
Rum, i.e. Asia Minor, 42 and n. 1, 43, 54, 56–8, 60, 61, 75, 76, 78, 79, 85, 89
Rum, Kisra of: (descendant of Salm and father of Katayun), 42–7; 58; (Failakus = Philip of Macedon), 60, 61; 75–7, 79; 85, 90, 93
Rushanak, or Roxana, wife of Sikander, 62–4
Rustam, son of governor of Khurasan, 98
Rustam, son of Zal and Rudaba, husband of Tahmina and father of Suhrab, 19, 23–7, 38–40, 52

Sakila, Mount, 46
Salm, son of Faridun and Shahrinaz, 13, 42
Sam, ruler of Zabulistan, 14, 18, 19
Samangan (Saminkan or Siminjan), 23 and n.
Sapinud, wife of Bahram Gur, 81–3
Sasan, 68, 96
Sasanian dynasty, founding of, 71
Sasanian period, 2; stories of, 73–99
Shabdiz, favourite horse of Khusrau Parwiz, 92
Shahrinaz, wife of Faridun, 10, 13, 42, 52; called Savanghavach in the Avesta, 10; Darmesteter's Çavanhavāc, 10 n.
Shangul, Indian King, 80–2
Shapur, or Sapor II, King of Iran, 75–9, 97

Shirin, Princess, wife of Khusrau Parwiz, 89–95
Shirwi, or Kubad, son of Khusrau Parwiz and Maryam, 93, 94, 96
Sikander, or Alexander the Great, 60–4, 71
Simurg, fabulous bird, 14
Sindukht, Queen of Kabul, 18
Sistan, 49
Sita, 52
Siyawush, son of Kai Kaus, husband of Farangis, 31–3
Sudaba, stepmother of Siyawush, 31
Suhrab, son of Rustam and Tahmina, 24–30

Tahmina, Princess of Samangan, wife of Rustam and mother of Suhrab, 23, 24, 27
Taq-i-Bustan, 92, 95
Teheran, 67 n. 2
"True Cross", the, 97
Tur, son of Faridun and Shahrinaz, 13
Turan, 25, 32, 35–8, 48, 50, 51, 82
Turkistan, Chinese, see Chin
Tus, birthplace of Firdausi, 1, 97
Tuwurg, chief of Khan of Chin, 87

Varahran V, see Bahram Gur
Verethraghna, the Yazata of Victory, 70 n.
Virgil, 104
Vishtaspa, see Gushtasp
Vullers, Firdusii, 9 n., 13 n., 19 n., 27 n., 30 n., 34 n.
Vullers-Landauer, Firdusii, 41 n.; 48 n., 52 n. 2, 59 n., 61 n.

Warner, The Shāhnāma of Firdausī, 8 n., 31 n., 33 n., 52 n.1, 54 n. 1, 57 n., 63 n., 94 n., 97 n. 1, 98 n.

West, Dr, 53 n. 2

White Castle, the, 25, 28

Yazdagird, or Isdegird III, last of the Zoroastrian Emperors of Iran, 99

Yazdagird, father of Bahram Gur, 80

Zabul, 25

Zabulistan, 14, 19, 24

Zahhak, or Azhi Dahaka, King of Babylon and of Persia, 5–8, 10, 12, 13, 52

Zairivairi, *see* Zarir

Zal, son of Sam, husband of Rudaba and father of Rustam, 14–19, 23

Zarduhsht, *see* Zoroaster

Zarir, 44 n., 47, 48; called Zairivairi in the *Avesta*, 47, 50

Zhanda Razm, 25

Zoroaster, or Zarduhsht, 48, 49, 62

For EU product safety concerns, contact us at Calle de José Abascal, 56–1°,
28003 Madrid, Spain or eugpsr@cambridge.org.

www.ingramcontent.com/pod-product-compliance
Ingram Content Group UK Ltd.
Pitfield, Milton Keynes, MK11 3LW, UK
UKHW010048140625
459647UK00012BB/1693